It's Up to You

You

Success Starts at Home

───────── ★ ─────────

Leslie Youra

BOUND
PUBLISHING

Bound Publishing

United States
6501 E. Greenway Pkwy
#103-480
Scottsdale, AZ
85254

Canada
Suite 114
720 28th St. NE
Calgary, AB T2A 6R3

Toll Free Phone and Fax: 1-888-237-1627
Email: info@boundpublishing.com
Web: www.boundpublishing.com

ISBN: 978-0-9867762-7-4

Cover: Lloyd Arbour
Text: Anamarie Seidel; Finely Finished LLC
Edit: Lynda Masterson; Valyn Enterprises LLC

ACKNOWLEDGMENTS

Books are not simply written; instead they grow inside our hearts and minds and with help from supportive family members and friends come to life. I want to express my gratitude to all of them here for their encouragement and inspiration.

First, I want to acknowledge my husband, Rick Youra and my children, Daniel, Kyle and Kaitlyn, who taught me how to be a better person, let go of the small stuff and discover my true self. They taught me what true love really is.

Next, I want to thank my two brothers, Dave and Dan Moore, their wives and my nephew for their expertise, advice, friendship and encouragement. I also want to thank my parents Larkin and Erma Moore for their love, support and guidance. Their lives, values, work habits, passion and fearlessness continue to serve as a model for my own life.

One of the best parts of writing this book was having the opportunity to work with Bound Publishing and others. Many wonderful people have worked closely with me to make this book a reality. I am especially grateful to Todd Dean, Scotty Prysko, Anamarie Seidel, Dick Nichols, Liz Ragland and Dee Burks who offered professional insights, guidance, understanding and good humor throughout the project. Thanks to all of you for a job well done.

Finally, to those parents who believe they really can create the life of their dreams, make a difference and strive to constantly improve themselves in order serve as outstanding role models for their kids, I say well done. You are the real reason I have written this book. Keep learning, keep growing and keep being a blessing to your children.

TABLE OF

CONTENTS

★

CHAPTER 1

THEY'RE A REFLECTION OF YOU

———————— ★ ————————

Parenting can be both challenging and rewarding. What's more, the older our children get the more difficult it becomes, especially in the case of teenagers. As a mother of three, I know firsthand the trials and rewards we face as parents. The trend in parenting today is to treat our children as equals in the home and let them find themselves. While I agree with giving children the freedom to find who they want to be, I don't believe that it has to come at the cost of the parents' sanity. Children, no matter their ages, need boundaries. *It's Up to You* will discuss how to support and guide your children through to adulthood.

I don't believe we should mollycoddle our children. I was raised to be self sufficient and independent and I in turn am raising my children in the same manner. The examples we set as parents, positive and negative, paint the canvas that our kids carry into adulthood. We can color their world with unwavering faith and a strong set of values or smudge it with uncertainty. Faith and values aren't instantaneous. We can't just download them onto our children like we do with a song on ITunes. Instead, faith and values must be learned and are a lifetime journey of self discovery, critical thinking, deepening commitments, and trusting relationships. Our children are watching us like hawks; therefore it is up to us to model exemplary behavior. Understanding this is important to parents who want to teach their children to live according to their own convictions in today's challenging environment.

Our children are the future and we should set the best example possible for them. Life is meant to be lived with energy, fueled by inspiration and the understanding that there are no limits. Stop and think about the magnitude of this. What would happen if you lived life to the fullest? Spent every day as if it were your last? What type of effect would this have on your children? I want to help you make the most out of your parenting.

This book will demonstrate that being a good parent starts with living the values that you want to instill in your children. You cannot truly teach your children anything that you cannot do for yourself. Therefore, this book focuses on self-improvement as much as it does on parenting techniques, so that you can implement the important lessons that you live and breathe in your own life. We will start by looking at five overarching ideas.

1. Start with yourself: five elements of a good life.
2. Construct a positive change
3. Accept responsibility
4. Build character
5. Set an example

START WITH YOURSELF:
FIVE ELEMENTS OF A GOOD LIFE

To begin with, we all want to give our children the tools to live a good life. In order to do that, we must figure out how to have a good life for ourselves, and then, by extension, our families.

In order to build this good life, you start by examining who you are, and what you truly want. From these, your most fundamental desires and beliefs, you can begin to develop your definition of a good life, both personally and professionally. For most people a good life consists of five elements; 1) health, 2) spirituality, 3) relationships, 4) intellectual and personal growth, and 5) financial well being.

Finding the right balance in your body, spirit, family, life and business will help you refine your goals, head in the right direction, and feel an all-around sense of well-being. All five elements must play a part, but in certain stages of our lives some have a more dominant part than others. I find I can only focus closely on two or three elements at any one time without feeling stress and frustration. I like to keep a chart of my progress in order to ensure that I work on all five elements throughout the year. Not only is this a great way to help me feel balance in my life, but it also creates a living record of my progress, successes and challenges.

HEALTH: BODY AND MIND

COMMITMENT ★ Decide to get in shape

INITIATIVE ★ Call a trainer

OPTIMISM ★ I know I can look & feel better

ACTION ★ 3 times a week

ACHIEVEMENT ★ Lost 9 pounds in one month

SPIRITUAL: LIFE AND SPIRIT

COMMITMENT ★ Want to get closer to God

INITIATIVE ★ Discovered classes at church

OPTIMISM ★ I know if I seek God, He will seek me

ACTION ★ Sign up for a class

ACHIEVEMENT ★ Met 28 other fantastic women who are seeking a closer relationship with God

If you can maintain a strong connection to these five elements, and you continue to nurture of them in your life, you will set the tone for a healthy, thriving environment for your children. No matter how young your children are, they will absorb the sense of a conscious, mindful approach to living that your example will set. These same five elements will play a big role in your children's own lives and they can start to learn about them at a young age. If you live a healthy life, for example, your children will learn to eat well and to be active. They can learn about your spiritual or philosophical values, and the role that these play in life.

Relationships will be strengthened as you work on keeping your own ties with family and friends, and your children will learn to communicate and relate to other people. Personal growth will play a central role, arising during the childhood years from a combination of their formal education and growing life experience. Even financial and work responsibilities can be taught early, by teaching the value of hard work, and teaching children to manage their own allowances and small savings accounts. These lessons can only be taught by experience, so start with you—take charge of these five elements in your life.

Construct a Positive Change

Stop for a moment and take a look at your life. Are you satisfied? Do you jump out of bed each morning with excitement to start the day? Or is your life flat, at a stalemate? Do you stare into space some days wondering when or if anything different is going to happen? Do you wake up each morning and just go through the motions? If you do, then it's time to examine your habits. Are you in control or are they controlling you?

Our habits are recurring, automatic patterns of behavior. If you think about how much of your life is made up of daily habits, or how many habitual thoughts occupy your mind every waking moment, you'll realize that they make up a significant part of your life. Habits are an important part of everyone's life, because habits allow us to complete regular tasks without having to figure out each action as if we were trying it for the first time.

But we also must remember to question regularly whether our habits still fit within our lifestyle. Good habits that are overworked or applied at the wrong time in our lives can become negative ones. For example, I have always liked my living space to be tidy, but once I had kids, it was not always possible. In the beginning, I tried hard to maintain order and was always frustrated and upset when I couldn't. However once I was able to accept that life gives us each challenges to help us grow, and that the house, car and kids did not always have to be neat and tidy, I was able to relax and find joy again. It wasn't the kids or the mess that was making me unhappy, it was just the rules I had developed growing up, and that needed to be modified when my life entered a new phase.

Productive habits give rise to efficiency, structure, stability, and security. Good daily habits are really the exercise of self-discipline. If you get up and go to work every day, focus on staying in motion to get things done, and fill your time with patience, persistence, and effort, you will reap the rewards.

On the other hand, destructive habits such as negative self talk, poor communication, overeating, smoking, drinking or procrastination can be self-defeating and have a negative pull on your self-esteem and self-worth. This, in turn, will affect all aspects of your life, from your personal accomplishments to the influence that you have on your family. A discernible percentage of your time is taken up with bad habits is time that you will not be devoting to worthwhile endeavors.

If you have been running on autopilot, you are probably acting on habit rather than conscious conviction. If this is the case, your habits are eating up your time, instead of increasing your efficiency to serve your larger goals. However if you find yourself in this situation, you can still construct a positive change in your life. You can create new habits. For example, you can make time to regularly take stock, gauge your progress, and decide to make new efforts toward improving your life.

Instead of adhering to mindless routines, make a habit out of thinking about how you are spending your time and whether your daily activities are moving you toward achievement, or are simply keeping you stuck. Instead of habitually coasting by without thinking, learn to live consciously, ensuring that each day brings you some new fulfillment. Habits should be the day-to-day work of moving toward ever-increasing happiness and meaning, and not merely a way to kill time or to get through a day. There should really be no conflict between your habits and your active mindset. Habit and routine should form the consistent daily basis of behavior that adds up to something much bigger.

If you want to make changes in your life, the basic switch you need to make is to get engaged in your day-to-day activities, instead of just running in place. There should be an active, dynamic sense of striving to make your days add up to more than simply getting by. Form new habits—not only healthier ones, but more mindful ones. For example, make it a habit to regularly sit down and think about whether you are accomplishing your goals, about whether you are happy, and about what you want to be working for. Then, form action plans to make your visions come to life.

If you do this, you will not only live a happier life for yourself, but you will also energize your family. You can demonstrate for your children the steps that it takes to make any dream come true. Your own positive attitude will rub off on everyone around you. Furthermore, taking an active approach to change and conscious living will allow you to see how your own habits and modes of functioning will affect your children.

Children absorb your behaviors, speech, and attitude like sponges. If you walk through your life on autopilot, making resolutions but never changing, they will absorb this passive attitude.

I have always been a bit of a perfectionist. That never seemed like a problem until I started to notice the habit in my daughter. I would see her afraid to try something new for fear of not knowing how, or not doing it well. Unfortunately, my bad habit had rubbed off on her and it is hard to break a habit once it is formed. If you take the time to note how you are living, and to strive to improve yourself, so will your children, because they will see the possibilities and the outcomes.

No one is perfect and I'm sure you noticed a few bad habits on both of the lists. But don't worry. You can change them. Take slow deliberate steps to make the change and encourage yourself and your family along the way. Make this a family affair. Start now, rather than tomorrow or next week. It doesn't have to be January 1st for you to make a resolution. For every moment that we wait, our children wait too.

ACCEPT RESPONSIBILITY

When you make a choice to change a certain area of your life, you must be accountable for the results or outcomes—both good and bad. Most people want success but aren't willing to make major changes in their lives to ensure it. It is very difficult to take an objective look at what is and isn't working in our lives, and to reach a targeted, specific plan for change.

To truly take personal responsibility in life you need to have the courage of your convictions and be able to let go of any concerns or judgment over how others live and what potential impact they might have on your family. In my case, I had to let go of the negative comments I heard when I decided to home school my son. "How are you qualified?" "Your son will be socially isolated." "Four-year colleges won't accept home schooled children." And so on. I took action and responsibility for my decision to improve my son's education. He has since graduated and is working full time at a job he loves. You need to own your emotions without blaming others for the way you feel, which of course sounds simpler than it actually is.

We can't go through life blaming our problems on circumstances, situations, or other people. This victim mentality causes us to blame anyone, everyone and everything for that which we are or are not doing. Our attitude changes to the point that we are only focused on ourselves and we develop a bitter attitude toward life. As I mentioned earlier, our children are like sponges in that they absorb everything in their environment. If they're constantly subjected to negativity and an "it's not my fault" attitude, how do you think they're going to handle the situations that occur in their lives?

Responsibility means accepting accountability for your successes and failures. Accountability is vital to moving beyond mediocrity and the status quo and toward achieving extraordinary results. People who are stuck in seemingly inescapable ruts sometimes find temporary relief in blaming everybody except themselves. They refuse to take responsibility for their inadequacies, readily blaming their education or lack of it, their upbringing, their employer, the economy, the government—the list is endless. It doesn't really matter where blame is placed, because placing responsibility anywhere outside of yourself means giving up personal control over your life.

Taking responsibility means accepting that ultimately we are in charge of our own lives. One of the outstanding traits of successful people is that they accept responsibility for themselves and refuse to blame others for their condition in life. Achieving this personal characteristic is an ongoing process. Every day we are faced with decisions that need to be made, obligations that must be agreed to or kept. They include the simple obvious ones, such as getting up in the morning and choosing to go into work or school as well as the harder decisions like staying in a particular marriage or job, or choosing what career to pursue after school is completed.

It becomes very easy to continue putting off until tomorrow those items which we find tedious or uncomfortable, and before we know it, weeks, months, and years have gone by and our dreams remain unfulfilled. This is a vicious cycle because, as the disappointments and frustrations mount, the harder it is to look back and take responsibility for mediocrity, blankness, and lack of progress. The good news is that it is never too late to make a positive change. Every day you wake up alive, you have the chance to take charge and be accountable.

So what are we responsible for anyway? While we cannot control many events, situations, or the actions of others, we are always responsible for three areas of our life:

★ Our attitudes - Even in bad situations, we can still control our attitudes. Granted, we don't have control over every stray thought that goes through our heads, or every flicker of emotion that events might give rise to, but our overall mindset (attitude) is something that is within our power. Essentially, an attitude is a way of approaching a situation. People with positive attitudes don't necessarily expect everything to always go well; it is not unrealistic or blind optimism that affects attitudes. Rather, someone with a good attitude looks for the best possible alternatives, and for ways to bring them about.

★ Our choices - Each of us is given the power of choice in our lives. Yet we often and too easily give up this power. Seizing control of our choices is one powerful way to take responsibility for our lives. In fact, relinquishing control, feeling helpless, and blaming other people or circumstances for what happens to us is in itself a choice. It's a poor choice that leads to unhappy results, but it is a choice nonetheless. Fortunately, we can always make better choices.

★ Our actions - Because we have the power of choice, we have control over the actions we choose to take. Although we don't have control over many of the circumstances that might arise in life, we are always responsible for the actions that we take in response to these circumstances. We are in control of all of our actions, large and small, every day.

Learning to take responsibility can be a challenging lesson, but once you understand this concept, you are empowered to make the correct decisions to move forward in life. We all have the ability to change the pattern of our everyday lives. Choice enables you to create your life, and taking responsibility for all of those choices empowers you to teach your children to do the same.

When you take responsibility for your actions, the mode of living that you demonstrate for your children is a priceless learning opportunity for them. And although children are not often in a position to fully make their own decisions, they can and will observe the ways that you make yours. You can also construct controlled and safe parameters within which your children can make limited decisions. As they get older, they will be able to take on wider and more important responsibilities.

BUILD CHARACTER

How do we build character? To build anything, it must have a foundation. Just as there are concrete foundations for homes and buildings, there are foundations—abstract rather than concrete—on which human character is built. The foundation of human character is a set of values. What values do you hold? In my family, we talk about the importance of honesty, integrity, forgiveness, generosity, caring, conservation, respect for the earth and other forms of life. Values are the defining factors that determine whether or not we succeed, and the road that we take to get there. If our actions aren't based on our values then we experience discomfort, confusion, and a lack of confidence. Living your life according to a set of strong values gives you freedom from fear and doubt because you know that you're acting according to your beliefs.

Everything we do and say in some way can be traced back to our values. For example, how do you decide what church is best for you and your family, what movie to see on Saturday night, what activities to engage in, what company to keep, what to wear, etc? Values give all of us the power to determine our destiny.

Our values can be consciously chosen, built into a system that contains no contradictions, and is conscientiously acted upon. On the other hand, our values might have been absorbed passively, the result of refusing to do the work of thinking for ourselves. In this case, our values will be a random collection, absorbed through chance, whim, or whatever influences come into our lives, and will be full of contradictions, weak, and will provide no comfort and only poor guidance at best. But however our values are absorbed, and whether they are good or bad, our thoughts, words, and actions are caused by some set of guiding principles.

Our thoughts, words, and actions in turn add up to a sum, and that sum is the essence of who you are—in other words, it is your character. Choosing our character and setting high standards for ourselves is what determines the life we live and it is always a personal choice. Each day we need to ask ourselves, "Am I living a life that is in alignment with my values?"

As a parent, it can be a difficult job to instill values in your children. We can't be with our kids 24/7 so we have to rely on the strength of the values we teach them. Your children will be exposed to many new experiences that will challenge their values. Peer pressure to engage in destructive or otherwise unhealthy pastimes can be overwhelming, strong values, however, can be the difference between yes and no.

Nothing is more important than a strong family foundation built on values and principles. Be a strong leader. Model your values and principles by living them daily. Instill in your children the idea that values and principles are non-negotiable and morals are not subject to popularity. Teach them the value of learning, how to discuss and share their ideas with love and respect, and how to stand up for what is right, even when it is not popular. Teach lessons that stay with them for life, which they can use and pass down to their children. Give them the proper foundation upon which they can build their own strong characters.

SET AN EXAMPLE

What would happen if you worked each day on the things that we have talked about so far? Imagine yourself living and working on the five elements of a good life as a regular, normal routine. You would continually strive to gain new heights in your health, your spirituality or values, your interpersonal relationships, your personal growth, and your financial success. Regardless of temporary setbacks or failures, if you never stop trying to reach new goals in these areas, you are bound to succeed in the long run.

Your accomplishments will also depend on the other ideas that have been discussed so far. You cannot continue to grow and change unless you practice being mindful about your habits, so that you are able to construct positive changes in your life. You also will need to practice the mental habit of accepting responsibility, which will put you in the driver's seat in all areas of your life, from home to work to your inner life. Finally, taking charge of your own character, in the form of choosing and living out your values, will give you the means to choose the best and healthiest goals.

If you practice all of these principles, you will possess the keys to success, happiness, and balance in both your inner, intangible being, and in the outer, visible areas of life. You will be a happy, healthy person who knows how to confront obstacles and to enjoy the fruits of your labor. But only by living like this, being fully engaged in your goals and values, can you really pass on these lessons to your children. You will be a constant example and a role model for your children. In a sense, everything that we have discussed so far, and that we will be discussing throughout this book, is about setting an example by acting on the principles that you want to teach. But it is worth discussing separately here, as a reminder of the importance of truly starting with yourself, and then passing on the lessons of experience to your children.

One of our primary objectives as parents should be acting as great, positive role models ourselves because we can't depend on anyone else to do so. There's no doubt about it, kids learn values, as well as other life skills, from their parents. As a parent, regardless of the words that come out of your mouth, it is your actions that your children really pay attention to. You can profess up and down how strongly you believe in education or ethics, but if you arrive home straight from work and turn on the TV instead of helping with homework, they'll get the message that you don't want them to hear: "Take the easy way out in life." If you want them to learn and prosper, then set a good example and make time to interact with them. Our goals as parents are to teach our children to make sound choices when they are out in the world. The pathway to a confident child starts with the bridge between parents and their children.

Our children are an extension of us, so the next time you look in the mirror, think about what you see. Is the person staring back at you someone you are proud of? Are your professional and personal lives the way you want them to be? No matter whether the answer is yes or no, one fact is undeniable. Harvey Firestone, executive of Firestone Tires, said it well: "You get the best out of others when you get the best out of yourself."

I believe this is especially true for us as parents.

Parents often express a desire for their children to have advantages that they (the parents) never had. This idea might be applicable to certain opportunities that a good financial situation or a healthy home life can provide. But, when it comes to character, values, communication, and coping skills, parents can really only teach children lessons that they have learned themselves. The "do as I say, not as I do" mentality simply won't cut it—you can't teach a single value or life skill with this approach. You must be the personification of happiness, health, and success that you want your children to learn to become. This book will provide you with some of the tools that you need to become this living, breathing example. The rest is up to you.

EXERCISE

Making changes requires not only that you visualize what you want in the future, but also that you take a good hard look at where you are now. Don't come back to this after finishing the book or the chapter; do it now. Off the top of your head, brainstorm the first habits that you can think of, whether brushing your teeth every day, to how you cook dinner. Then, list habits that you see in your children.

YOUR DAILY HABITS	YOUR CHILD'S HABITS
1.	1.
2.	2.
3.	3.
4.	4.
5.	5.
6.	6.
7.	7.
8.	8.
9.	9.
10.	10.

How do you feel when you look at each of your present habits? Which ones are productive? Are there any on the list that no longer serve you or that prevent you from reaching a goal? Do you see any of your habits you listed above surface in your children? Is it beneficial to their lives?

Chapter 2

Outside Influences

———————— ★ ————————

Our children pick up new information every day. This information comes from the sources that should directly influence them, like parents and teachers. However, there are also many other influences in their lives. They have extended family members and family friends. They encounter new people regularly, and their peers will affect them in both good ways and bad. They also have access to almost any and every bit of data floating through the air, through all of the various communications media that are available to them.

In this chapter, we will discuss these outside influences, and two ways of approaching them. The first is the perspective of the interaction between your influences and outside influences. As always, the real lessons start with you, the parent. In the first section we will devote some discussion to preparing for outside influences by instilling good values of your own:

1. A Solid Foundation

The second perspective discusses some ways in which you can have some control over what outside influences actually have an effect on your child. You can guide your kids to make good choices in their lives even as they try to become more independent. The second two sections address this topic:

2. Some Thoughts on the Media

3. Extended Families and Beyond—Mentors

At the end of the chapter is an exercise to get your active approach started.

Many parents fall into a mode of thinking of all outside influences as negative, and about arming their children against all the bad of the world. This is valid, of course, but it is equally important that your children learn to open themselves up to all of the good opportunities and knowledge out there. Take a balanced approach, and teach yourself and your children to distinguish between the two.

A SOLID FOUNDATION

Outside influences often exercise a strong pull over teens, and can seem to dilute the values we want to teach our children, but children are also influenced by the relationships in their lives, especially the parent-child relationship. Whether they admit it or not, deep down they need you and appreciate the idea that you want to create a relationship. It's true that during the teenage years they will want to spread their wings. With all of the activities children are engaged in today, you may be living according to a schedule that makes the bonding experience much more difficult. It's important that you do everything you can to overcome these obstacles and find a way to form a strong foundation from the outset by building a relationship with your child that is based on common values, interests, passions, etc.

Here is a quick overview of some of the "big picture" ideas that you need to keep in mind amid all of the distractions of daily existence.

★ Set guidelines. One reason for a deteriorating relationship is that your children may not know what is expected of them, so be specific. Be consistent in enforcing your rules. Do not waver; your child must know that you will keep your word.

★ Act as a role model. No matter how old your children are, they still look to you for guidance. In the first chapter we talked about how they mimic your actions more than they follow your words. In talking with my husband recently over lunch, he was saying how important it is for him to continually model behaviors he wants to see in our children. For example, if he wants more affection and closeness with the children he has to be more affectionate and initiate more contact. If he wants the children to eat healthier, he has to make better food choices when we go out together. If he wants the children to have a great work ethic, he has to make work a priority and do great work. If he wants the children to be loyal to each other and the family, he has to support them and only speak of their strengths with others. We each have the ability to influence our families either by our positivity or negativity. It is important to remember that children notice everything.

We can't rely on outside sources to give our children a solid foundation for success. We need to start at home. The relationships we build with our children provide a buffer between their home and external environments.

Our children have greatness in them, and we can give them the confidence to make the right choices when they walk out the door. Children will only come into their own, develop along the right lines and be open with you if you teach them the proper values to begin with. We have discussed this before and will continue to do so throughout this book. You need to instill values in your children from an early age, and the only way to truly teach them is to practice them yourself. You should know exactly what your values are and you should pursue them openly and with enthusiasm.

There are resources for looking at values and making them a real, concrete part of your life. For example, I like Roy Posner's many discussions of the roles that values play in people's lives.

Posner makes lists of values for different aspects of life: for example, personal, business, and societal values. These kinds of writings can help us stay more conscious of and focused on the specific principles and ideas that we want to work on and to keep active in our lives. The clearer our own ideas about what are the important things and how to act on them become, the better we can pass these ideas on to our children. Only when you have a clear idea of what your values are can you model them for someone else.

Let's look at a few examples of values from Posner's list. Out of the many concepts, he includes discipline, honesty, and health/well-being. These are among the most common principles, and probably most people would agree that these are good and important ideas. Beyond that, however, how well can most people define and lay out strategies and practices for each of these values? And, how well do most people practice these ideas without compromise or equivocation? Although the rightness of values seems indisputable when they are talked about directly, actually applying them in practice becomes a much more complicated endeavor than one might at first think.

★ Discipline, for example, can be a tough one to maintain. Most people have areas where they practice good discipline, and other areas where they never seem to establish and maintain good routines. For example, many people manage to get up every day, having enough discipline to get themselves to work and their children to school. However, when it comes to exercising, some people never do seem to maintain a new regimen for longer than a few weeks before the new good health resolutions collapse.

★ This is not to say that no one should ever get a break in any area. But whatever you emphasize, your kids will pick up on. So having discipline is in itself a value, and so is the ability to prioritize and practice discipline in a balanced way in all of the areas of life that you truly find worthwhile. The basic values, like discipline, that form the basis of many other values and have wide-ranging effects in life, are really only learned by children in a natural and uncomplicated manner if they see these values in practice as a normal part of life.

★ Honesty is another such value. When put in plain, up-front terms, I don't believe I've ever heard anyone who did not agree that honesty is a very important value, or who did not become angry upon finding out that they have been lied to. However, how many people do you know who are fully honest at all times, without any exceptions? In practice, it's not so straightforward, is it? It's important to define for yourself, in strict terms, what such values mean to you, and to not cross any lines without acknowledging your mistakes.

★ If you lie to your children, they'll feel betrayed and any trust you've established will be lost. Besides if you lie, doesn't it make it okay for them to lie as well? Your teens don't need to know all the details of every incident of your life, but don't hide or skim over important issues. When asking your opinion on any subject, your answer may not be one they want to hear, but knowing that you gave them an honest answer helps them to trust you. And watching you tell the truth to other people, even when it is uncomfortable, will show them honesty in practice.

★ Health and well-being might be a more straightforward thing to demonstrate in many ways, but many people don't succeed at this in their own lives. Poor eating and exercise habits are definitely passed on from one generation to the next. People who don't learn while young how to eat healthy and to stay active and address specific health concerns often have grave difficulties with their health and self-esteem when they reach adulthood, and they fight a losing battle their whole lives with these issues.

★ On the other hand, people who grow up learning good habits from the start have a much easier time maintaining health and well-being. It is extremely difficult for adults who have never had healthy habits to adopt a new lifestyle. Healthy living takes knowledge, commitment, and discipline. If your children grow up learning these things, they will feel natural. If they grow up in an unhealthy atmosphere, a healthy lifestyle might seem unattainable.

Even when we are talking about outside influences, it is important to start at home, with ourselves, in our own lives.

SOME THOUGHTS ON THE MEDIA

Television, the internet, and the ever-evolving progression of telecommunications allow instant access to ideas to a degree unprecedented in human history. It has become a popular way of thinking to blame technology and the media for every one of the ills of modern society. This habit is both short-sighted and impractical. Short-sighted, because it allows us to take for granted the immense benefits that technology brings to all areas of life, from work to education. Using technology responsibly lets people work, communicate, educate themselves, and stay informed at a pace and a level that people in an earlier age, no matter how strong their thirst for knowledge and discovery, could not possibly aspire to. Technology-bashing is also impractical, because these influences are not going anywhere, and complaining about them will not help your children navigate the modern world. In addition, blaming outside influences, including the media, for poor or lazy behavior in our children is an excuse not to take full responsibility for the way we live and raise our families.

But we do need to acknowledge that along with good ideas and information come plenty of bad ideas, mindless exchanges, and false, misleading, worthless, and time-wasting bits of data. These things present parents with a need to be more vigilant than ever about monitoring how children spend their time. Parents also need to arm their children with the means to evaluate all of this information, and to choose the right interactions, whether virtual or real-world.

The average child uses some form of entertainment media as much as 53 hours each week. Worse still, many adults spend more time using media then they spend working. It is imperative that parents act as role models because change starts at the top. If we do not commit to change we cannot expect our children to change either.

The Kaiser Family Foundation determined through a research program on children's exposure to media that:

★ 83% of children under 6 years old participate in some form of screen media including TV, internet, DVD's, video games or cell phones.

★ Before children enter kindergarten, they have each watched 4,000 hours of TV.

★ They are exposed to 20 to 25 acts of violence per hour on Saturday morning TV on programs intended for children

★ Children ages 8-18 spend on average 7 hours and 38 minutes per typical day with media-- that's a whopping 53 hours a week!

Violence, sex, scandal, death and destruction not only infiltrate our children's minds through the media, internet and video games but are glorified by them as well. Many media images have also given our children a predefined notion of success and beauty. Both male and female models sell everything from milk to clothes to cars. The beauty industry is enormously profitable. The problem is that advertisers are also lining their pockets with the damaged self esteem of both youth and adults who sometimes lack the skills to put these images into perspective. We don't need to perfect our bodies; instead we need to perfect our minds.

Along with unrealistic body images, the media can give contradictory, unrealistic, and dangerously trend-driven information about sex. The presence of misinformation in advertising stereotypes is disturbing, given the research that indicates young people often turn to media for information about sex and sexuality. Approximately two-thirds of young people turn to media when they want to learn about sex, according to a study conducted in 2003 by David Buckingham and Sara Bragg.

Violence in the media has a further negative impact on our children. Think about how many images of death, and how many stories of murder, rape, and theft we see and hear on the news each night. The news, of course, is merely the tip of the iceberg. The color, excitement, and graphic images of the media can have a strong affect on children who are lacking stronger real-life influences. A study conducted by Kaiser Family Foundation found that nearly half of parents with children aged four to six report that their children have imitated aggressive behaviors from television.

Let me state again that not all media is bad; as a matter of fact it can be a powerful positive tool for learning and entertainment. But you do have to be selective and observant about the type and amount of exposure your children have to these influences. Instead of allowing our children to be influenced by the negativity, let's give them something positive to focus on. Teach yourself and your children to seek out educational outlets and ways to use the media that engage the mind. Let them see the pursuit of knowledge, kindness, gratitude, heroism, tolerance, and integrity in their entertainment and virtual communication.

Extended Families and Beyond—Mentors

If you work hard to lay this type of solid foundation, your kids will be well on their way to building a happy and successful life for themselves as adults. Your influence as a parent is the earliest and strongest that they will feel. But there will always be outside influences as well, and these will become increasingly important to your children as they get older and enter their teen years. They will be able to see for themselves that the values you teach at home are not always practiced in the outside world. They will come into contact with examples of other values, and of examples of amoral and immoral behavior all around them. It is important to let your kids understand that although not everyone practices the values that you teach, they can pursue their own paths, and that integrity is a key to long-term happiness.

Rather than allow an "us-against-the-world" mentality to develop however, you can allow your children to see that there are other people who build their lives around values, and who succeed by doing so. As much as you influence your children, one of the primary needs of all children, especially teenagers, is the need to become independent of their parents. Think about when you were their age. Didn't you feel grown up and have a strong urge to do your own thing? During this time, you'll be tested to the limit, but remember that teens are growing up, and they do in fact need to establish their independence. You may be wondering how to balance having a close relationship with allowing your teenager to have the increased freedom and responsibility that they require in this stage between childhood and adulthood.

This is a tough balancing act, and you should maintain your overall authority and communication. But, you cannot always get them to tell you everything, and you certainly can't look over their shoulders every second. In fact, it would be extremely unhealthy for any teen *not* to make attempts to be self-directed during these years. When your teens seek independence, you need to realize that they are going to confide in someone, and this is why I believe it is so important for them to find a responsible mentor.

During these years, your children will start to define their own identities. This is where it is normal for teenagers to reject their parents' ideas, and opinions, and to question their values. Young children need guidance, and they increasingly turn to their peers for feedback, support and companionship. While their friends are very important, they obviously aren't always the best source of advice. We have to accept this fact without too much emotion and realize that if they can find a positive coach or mentor they can gain a new perspective on the world.

Teens that have had mentors are happier with their lives and are apt to make better choices, such as getting involved in the community, volunteering, staying off drugs and waiting to have sex. But finding a mentor is not easy. You can't just call your neighbors and ask them to spend the majority of their time with your child. For a lucky few, mentors can be found through a privileged network of relatives or family friends. For everyone else, the search requires patience, persistence, a clear focus and self-confidence.

Your first question might be, when should you start looking for a mentor? Once you start thinking about it, this becomes a more complicated question that it might seem at first. And, as with many questions in life—especially with parenting—there is no one-size-fits-all answer. In a nutshell, your children should seek mentors when they both need and want outside influences, and will be receptive to the steady commitment of an outside relationship. Of course the applicable criteria will vary depending on your family's and your child's needs. Here are a few questions and factors that might influence your decision:

★ If you have a child who has special needs that are hard for you to keep up with, or that prevent your child from being receptive to parental authority, then you might decide to seek a mentor for your child starting from a very young age. If this is the case, there are mentorship programs and information that specialize in particular areas. For example, do a web search for "mentor ADHD" or "find a mentor child Asperger's", and you will find that there are many resources out there for you.

★ Look for signs that your child, 'tween, or teen is beginning to actively seek out other influences. For example if your child becomes less communicative with you, spending more time alone or with friends, then your input as a parent might not be fulfilling your child's need for instruction and example any longer. While this can feel hurtful, remember that the effort to become independent is—at bottom—a healthy impulse for a young person to follow. Instead of trying to rein this in, direct and help your child to find the right people to associate with.

★ If your family or your child is undergoing a major life transition, such as a move, an illness, a change of schools or any of the other things that can happen in life, your child might benefit from building relationships outside of the family.

★ Barring other factors, the early teen and high school years are a good time to begin thinking about mentorships. This is typically the age where children are actively seeking new ideas and trying to develop their own identities, but they are also very open to new people and relationships.

When you decide to begin this search, consider the potential benefits. Of course your child should reap the benefits of a supportive, knowledgeable voice in their life, and of a relationship outside the family. Time and again, successful people will describe the lasting effects that an early mentor has had on their lives, and the lessons instilled and opportunities afforded by such a connection.

But the effects can be much stronger and more lasting than that. There are the benefits experienced by the mentee as well. And you and the rest of your family can certainly benefit from the development of your teen into a better and brighter person. The advantages may continue to accrue and to spread in a ripple effect throughout the life of your child. Given a positive mentor experience, your teenagers might be encouraged to pass on the lessons that they have learned. Teens can receive the greatest benefit when they begin to give back. Teens who become a mentor for a peer or younger student not only reinforce their own learning, but also set themselves up as experts. When teens mentor another child they get to experience ownership of knowledge and respect that is usually reserved for adults only. And then the good effects are passed along to any mentees that your child decides to associate with.

Once you have decided that the time is right and you understand the benefits, you need to consider what qualities make a good mentor. At the very least, you need to find someone who will strengthen and reinforce the basic values that you want to instill. But you should not look for someone who is a carbon copy of you. While you want living examples of the good things that you are trying to instill, you also need to expose your child to new perspectives. Ultimately, only your teen can decide whom they will admire and respect enough to truly make the most of the mentor/mentee relationship. Frankly, this choice might be someone who is very different from you. Try to be objective about this choice, and don't let fears or your impulse to hold on to your "baby" get in the way. Remember that this is a step toward independence that should be encouraged.

Help your child understand the criteria that should be used when looking for a good mentor. Here are some good resources that can help you to be specific about the qualities that a mentor should have:

★ The Big Sister/Little Sister organization has put together a good write-up outlining the search for a mentor: *http://archive.ifla.org/IV/ifla74/papers/099-Cotera-en.pdf*

★ Here is a good basic list of good mentor qualities: *http://polaris.gseis.ucla.edu/jrichardson/documents/mentor.htm*

★ This page outlines finding a career mentor, but is also a good basic outline of desirable qualities to look for, and provides tips on finding a mentor that can be applied to teens' needs as well: *http://www.job-search-coach.com/what-makes-a-good-mentor.html*

Once you and your child understand what to look for, it's time to start your search, and then to ask the person that you (and your teen) decide on to be a mentor. If you attend church, and like and trust the community there, this is a great place to start. A church community, for example, can be the teen's home away from home, where they will most certainly find a mentor to guide them into becoming a productive and fulfilled adult.

You can also ask other parents or local school administrators. Try looking on networking sites such as *http://www.meetup.com* for groups and individuals in your area. Think of activities that your child enjoys and search for special programs built around them, whether it's a favorite sport, hobby, academic endeavor, or another type of group. There are other sources that you can use to find guidance and support for your teen. For an extensive international list of mentor programs, try *http://www.mentors.ca/mentorprograms.html.*

Here is an excellent page outlining ten steps to take when looking for a mentor (this is also directed to career mentorships, but is applicable to any situation): *http://powertochange.com/world/findmentor.* Another good how-to resource on searching for and asking someone to be a mentor is the following: *www.imdiversity.com/villages/careers/articles/whitehead_find_a_mentor.asp.*

When you are ready to approach the person that you and your child or teen have selected, you should be honest and straightforward. If your child is a teen, then your teen is the one who should do this. It might be nerve-wracking, but this is a step toward independence and should be treated as such. Furthermore, taking ownership of this step from the beginning will get your teen invested in this process, which is the only way for him/her to really reap the benefits. Help your child to work out the approach and keep it simple. Outline why you would like this person to become a mentor, what time and other commitments might be expected, and then simply ask. Don't underestimate what you can gain by simply asking for what you want—this is a very good lesson for your children.

For some inspiration, here is an article written by a mother whose recalcitrant child finally found a proper mentor. This is a real example of the benefits of a mentor/mentee relationship: *http://parenting.families.com/blog/teens-need-mentors.*

We can be infinitely greater tomorrow than we are today and most of us haven't even begun to tap into what we can accomplish. Help your child to expand your vision of their life, but allow them to create dreams of their own. All of us have limitless potential, and we all want to help our children reach theirs. If your child is surrounded by positive role models, and has a variety of resources in good times and in bad, they can emerge from these trying years as confident, capable young adults, ready for higher education, a career, and a life of adventure, productivity and personal fulfillment.

★

EXERCISE

On the next page create a list of social values. Conduct a search for "What are Society's Values" by Roy Posner. Define and discuss the different values from your list with your children. Chose your top five values and have your children do the same. Are they the same values? Discuss what it means to live your values and write down two or three actions you might take to incorporate your top values into your everyday life. We all have core values whether we realize it or not, and by taking the time to uncover and discuss those values we strengthen our relationships with our children and gain insight into who they are becoming.

SOCIAL VALUES

Parent	Child

Actions	Actions

CHAPTER 3

CONSIDER
THE POSSIBILITIES

─────────── ★ ───────────

Did you know that only 18 percent of employees today believe
that they are using their natural talents in their current careers?
Sadly, the majority of us work in jobs that don't require us to
use our innate talents and strengths. Identifying and using our
talents is central to the experience of living in fulfillment, since
most of us will spend most of our lives at work. Yet many of us
are uncertain of our talents, of how to discover them and of how
to use them.

The problem is that the term 'talented' is used to describe only
the most outwardly successful and intelligent people. They are
usually described as highly motivated and driven to succeed.
Does intelligence equal talent? No, not at all. A high IQ does not
automatically mean talent. In addition, even if you are driven,
you can be unsuccessful. Why? Because if you're in a job just
for the money, you're not going to be happy. Money can only
take you so far. So before we go any further, I'd like to point
out that money doesn't equal success. Truly successful people

are happy with all aspects of their lives. Stop for a moment and think about your career. Are you using your talents? Does your current job align with your strengths? If the answer is no, how can you be driven and motivated to succeed in a field you're not suited for?

I believe that every single person has talent, and that includes our children and teenagers. What that talent is and how it can be utilized is another matter. How can you help your children discover and develop their talents and find a calling in life that will lead them to fulfillment?

The word "talent" has been given so many different definitions that we may not even realize its true meaning anymore. According to the dictionary, talent is defined as a natural ability or aptitude. Notice the word 'natural.' When we refer to talent we're not talking about acquired or learned abilities. This is where the confusion lies. The Thesaurus associates talent with words such as gift, knack, capacity, adeptness, and brilliance. We are either born with a talent or not. When our children find their natural ability to do something well, they will live a truly fulfilled life. My son graduated recently and when I asked him what he wanted to do, he told me that wanted to spend his time finding what he likes to do. Now, some parents would rather hear an answer such as "go to college" or "get a job". Not me. I want my son (and my daughter as well) to find their natural talents and use them to their fullest. The place where talent and passion overlap is the jumping-off point for success and happiness in a big-picture sense.

FINDING OUR TALENTS

While I was involved in the field of education, I saw many of the so called 'best and brightest' identified as part of the talent. Meanwhile, the morale of the "non-talented" sank, many quit school or disengaged and as a result their performance suffered.

Every single one of us has a special talent and strength. Although yours may be different from that of your family, friends and co-workers, all are equally important. We have a responsibility to ourselves to discover what our talent is and as parents it is also our responsibility to help our children find their talents and strengths as well. Once children know their own strengths and talents, and understand how to put them to use, they can build confidence, follow their dreams, and create their futures. Schools are very good at teaching children about their weaknesses and helping them see what they cannot do and what they do not know, which is why it is so important for us as parents to help our children find what they love to do.

There are vast reserves of untapped potential residing in our children. When we acknowledge that and help them to find and foster this potential, everyone wins. We will ensure their success as adults if we start developing their abilities today. All children need to find and develop their talents, skills and intellect so they can live a fulfilled life. No one has written our children's destinies. They write their own and make their own futures. Every child is unique. All children have strengths and talents inside them, and yet there is the possibility that their uniqueness will go unrecognized.

When children discover and develop their talents and strengths they enter onto the path to happiness. When we work according to our talents, we feel vitalized and confident. We live with a sense of purpose, connectedness, resilience, and fulfillment. It is imperative to foster these traits in our children. But how is this done? Children are not that different from adults. They want clear and realistic goals, expectations for their futures and the ability to think for themselves in order to feel fulfilled and strong. When children go to a particular college or follow a career path just to please someone else, they end up living on autopilot and just going through the motions. No matter what their personalities or characteristics, children will not develop their true talents or discover their real strengths without a process of encouragement, nurturing, and sustained approval from those closest to them.

When children are encouraged to discover their uniqueness, they can begin to envision a future where they play a specific role. Children's strengths and talents are their own and are not for us to choose. Each person must understand his or her own talents and take responsibility for them. We can't choose them for our children, but we can provide an environment that is open and supportive of them while they discover them for themselves. As our kids enter the real world, they will need to be prepared to enter a workforce that is entirely different from the one we are in today.

Success 101

If we accept that talent is something that we are born with, surely we must know how to identify talent, and how to develop and apply it. But if that's the case, why don't we utilize our talents? This goes back to the way in which we were schooled. Were you taught to memorize facts so that you can pass some state-mandated test? Today, that is what is happening in the majority of our school systems. Robert Kiyosaki once said, "I suspect one reason they don't teach financial literacy in school is because our schools teach people to be employees." The truth of the matter is that schools don't offer any classes that train students for real life success.

In addition to the lack of necessary classes such as critical thinking, time management, and finance, the majority of public schools ignore bright children. My daughter is a classic example of this. One evening at dinner we were talking about school and she remarked that it is easier to be quiet and follow the crowd because the teachers tend to be stricter on students who think and act differently. Encouraging creative thinking is simply not on the agenda of the public schools. A student who wants or needs special attention must depend on individual faculty members—in some cases breaking school/union rules. From my experience, I believe that many public school systems have a conformity mindset rather than promoting exceptional, creative, independent thinkers.

Our experience with the public school system regarding our children is typical. My son's and daughter's stories are two of many. The system is designed from the top down to be a "one-size-fits-all" factory style grinder mass producing pre-designed citizens, not individuals inspired to find and nurture their natural talents. Students might emerge with a basic understanding of history, science, math and English but do they have the life skills necessary for success after graduation? School does not prepare children for life. Each year of school merely prepares them for the next year of school.

While public schools are required to "offer instruction" in a few basic subjects, there is no legal requirement for children to be forced to attend classes in which they are bored silly and which do not even give them the basic skills. For example, reading instruction has been changed from learning how to read using phonics, to guessing at words using a farce called Whole Language, resulting in massive reading failure. The same is true in math. The schools use "fuzzy math" instead of teaching how to calculate for correct answers. The business world and the professions are appalled at this massive failure.

A study by the Thomas Fordham Foundation (and others) provides a key to why so many people are choosing alternatives such as homeschooling for their children. It is that the standards of teaching in the public schools of America have long been poor and are steadily getting worse. What that means is that the quality of the teaching and the teachers has been falling for 50 years and continues to do so today. (Microsoft is forced to hire 200,000 people from overseas because American high school grads cannot read or write English adequately, or do simple math).

In order to provide the student body with the necessary basics, all students are required to participate in certain core classes that might or might not be of interest to them. With a lot of information to cover in a limited amount of time, teachers and students face the challenge of comprehension versus memorization. Schools go more toward memorization, rather than toward comprehending information. They memorize facts without understanding what those facts are all about. Memorization gets many people by in school, but how much do they actually retain and understand? In most cases students just memorize the necessary facts for the exam and then forget everything to cram for the next test a few days later. Children really need to know the information and how it applies. They also need to know how to express that application in writing. In life, they're going to be faced with situations and circumstances where rote facts can't help you. They have to be prepared to live according to a broader spectrum of information.

High school prepares teenagers for college, but not for real life, just as college doesn't completely prepare you for real life. There are certain skills that you need in the world that you aren't taught. There is no lesson that teaches you leadership, independence or self-reliance. For my son, the constant surveillance, rigid schedules and strict guidance imposed in high school inhibited his development at times. More freedom in high school can teach our children how to take responsibility for their time and themselves, as opposed to constantly having teachers telling them what to do.

My husband and I are advocates of homeschooling in all its forms, because our children can learn what, when, where and with whom they choose. Let your kids know that they are responsible for their lives and for their learning, and no one else is. The big advantage our children had, thanks to homeschooling, is that they learned to be in charge of their learning, and really their lives to a great degree. In contrast, kids who attend schools learn to wait for others to tell them what to do, what to think. After twelve years of that, they become completely dependent on others for direction.

We believe that homeschooling is the best preparation for the real world. In life, successful people have initiative and can motivate themselves, know what they want to learn and most importantly, know how to find information when they need it and are not afraid to make decisions for themselves. Those characteristics are the opposite of what public schools teach. The government schools have the goal of turning out a "workforce" of dependent predictable people. Our children, and many homeschooled children we know, learned to be independent and creative thinkers, to do what was right for them. Homeschooling almost always yields positive results since it reconciles the child's needs and interests with his or her life experience.

The corporate world reinforces the one-size-fits-all approach when companies hire based on grades and assume that this correlates with performance. In spite of overwhelming evidence that it does not, many companies continue with this practice. And in spite of overwhelming evidence that learning without reference to the employee's talents is unproductive, too many schools and curricula continue in this way.

WHAT ARE YOUR OPTIONS?

Children's academic performance shouldn't be judged specifically on achieving a predetermined score on a standardized test. The larger measure of their success involves whether they possess an overall and well-integrated foundation of knowledge— thinking skills such as creativity, intellectual assertiveness, and flexibility to use that knowledge effectively in real life situations. Rather than focusing on national content standards, students' opportunity for success increases when we make certain they have the above skills as well as possessing the values, character, habits, and interpersonal skills needed to achieve and exceed the demands of their future. With the developments in science and technology, along with the challenges of global economic competitiveness, we need to ensure that our children are well equipped with these types of critical thinking skills. Good is no longer acceptable. We have to give our children the foundation to excel in life.

Many parents believe that public school is the only choice they have for their children but more and more parents are opting for alternative education. Choosing a school for your children can appear to be an overwhelming and difficult task, especially when you realize that the schools you chose will have a big impact on your children's self-confidence, their ability to learn and their childhood experiences. The right decision can help them learn and overcome many barriers and difficulties they may have, while the wrong decision can have a tremendously negative impact on both their social and academic lives. There are many advantages and disadvantages to each option. All need to be examined and your decision should be based on what is right for each particular child. So what are your options? They include:

- ★ Public
- ★ Private
- ★ Charter
- ★ Home School

Each of these options has its own set of benefits and disadvantages. Which option will be best for you and your family? This depends on the child as well as the schools that are available to you in your local area. To determine which school is best, parents have to see what their child needs the most and which option is going to provide the best learning experience. Let's take a look at the different options in greater detail.

Public School Unlike private or charter schools, this option is free and is required to accept every student enrolled, which can cause overcrowded classrooms. Larger classrooms mean more students and less individual attention from teachers, which can translate into a lower quality education. The curriculum in public schools must also adhere to both state and federal regulatory standards. In most cases theological or religious studies aren't introduced into curriculum but we're starting to see a different trend occur in some schools.

The students in public school are also exposed to a variety of classmates from differing cultural and socio-economic backgrounds. This can have its disadvantages as well as advantages. Your children may be subjected to language and behavior you don't condone. But it can also be beneficial because it teaches children how to get along with one another regardless of differences. Public schools also offer a wide variety of subjects and extracurricular programs. If you feel that public school is the correct choice, find out how your school ranks statewide and nationally. Is it exemplary or unsatisfactory? It is also a good idea to schedule a meeting with the administration and tour the campus to help you and your child get a better feel for the school.

Private School Private school is a great option for many reasons including more individualized attention as well as religious education in some schools, if that is important to you. The class sizes are much smaller in private schools than in public schools. Smaller classrooms give students the advantage of learning the concepts of the various subjects in a more complete manner whereas public school students can fall through the cracks and move onto higher grades regardless of whether or not they learned the subject matter. However this extra attention comes at a price in that all private schools charge tuition. If this option doesn't fit into your budget, check to see if any scholarships are available.

In addition to a higher quality education, parents choose a private education for many other reasons, such as a safe, orderly environment and moral and ethical values similar to those taught in the home. The goal of a private school is to graduate a student capable of making a positive contribution to society. With more stringent rules and dress codes, private schools teach the students to be respectful to their elders and other people around them as well as basic life skills required to behave properly as a young adult in society. Parents also often look to private schools as an extension of the home in promoting the values and beliefs they embrace. To choose the right private high school for your child, make certain to thoroughly explore and understand the philosophy of the school.

Charter School Charter schools are tuition-free public schools that operate independently from the traditional school districts. The first charter school, opened in Minnesota in 1992, was designed to deliver programs tailored to educational excellence and the needs of the community. Since then more than 4,600 charter schools have opened across the United States by parents, educators, and civic leaders. People who are interested in improving the quality of learning but disagree with federal and state education mandates for conventional public schools are the main proponents for charter schools.

Public organizations fund charter schools and as a result, these schools are required to perform according to the contracts that support them. Charter schools operate as public schools, but are also similar to private schools in that the charter school sponsors have complete control over the curriculum.

Home Schools This option allows you to teach your children at home following an approved curriculum and lesson plans. There are many reasons that parents may opt to provide their children with a home school education. In my case, I felt that public schools weren't acceptable for my children--ethically, morally, mentally, and spiritually. The presence of a multitude of belief systems within the school and the bullying behavior exhibited by both the students and faculty was not something I wanted to subject my children to.

There are actually some good schools out there with caring, competent teachers, but they are becoming fewer and farther between. I prefer a home school education because private and home schools provide higher and more stringent academic standards and a safer learning environment than the public schools can offer.

There are disadvantages to home schooling too. Socialization is a primary concern of many parents who want to provide a home school education for their children. Public, private and charter schools still offer a much better environment for socialization, but homeschooling is making great strides in this area. With more and more parents opting to home school, associations are increasingly becoming more available allowing for home schooled students to interact with others, form sports teams, and have proms and class parties. If you decide to home school, socialize your child through clubs, sports and other extracurricular activities that will help develop the child's social skills. A solid home school education needs to fill in any social gaps in order to be most effective.

If you are interested in homeschooling, you can register with your local school district and receive standard expectations for your child's academic development. Public libraries, the Internet, and specialized home school education publishers and curriculums can help parents provide an adequate and effective home school education for their children. Laws regarding homeschooling vary from state to state, so be aware that many states want attendance records and expect that home-schooled children will participate in statewide standardized testing.

Each of these types of schooling can be a valid option, depending on the needs of your family. The choice is not an easy one. So if you are considering a public school because you can't afford tuition, a private school with smaller class sizes, a charter school that aligns with your personal values and beliefs or even home schooling so you can have more control over what your children learn, the best choice is the one that motivates your children and encourages them to strive for their personal best.

Regardless of which option we choose, ultimately what matters most is that our children are educated. So the best course of action is to do your homework and find out which method of schooling best fits your child's needs. Speak with the administration or local association and ask pertinent questions about what type of success they have with learning, student to teacher ratio, ranking, and how they handle behavior problems. Once you have a good idea about which option will be best, give it time to allow your children to settle in. Expect to see ups and downs for a time after the initial change. Even when we make the best choice, based on our children there may still be problems.

Our society longs for young people who are respectful and make a contribution to society in addition to being engaged students. I want my children to behave in a manner that creates a balanced life and allows them to achieve their dreams. Until we overcome our resistance to change, and place our primary focus on the success of our youth, we won't be able to prepare them for anything more than the status quo. Now is the time to make the decision that we are no longer going to accept what is transpiring in our classrooms. By taking a proactive step, we can immediately raise the standards for our children and give them the necessary tools to succeed in life. By raising standards, we are laying a path for upward advancement. The more we expect out of our children and the education system, the more we'll receive. Our children's successes will be in direct correlation to the level that we seek to attain. The higher we aim in life, the higher we get. Inevitably, the actions we take now will result in a dramatic change in the quality of the lives of our children.

★

Exercise

Make a list of all of the educational options in your local areas. Determine the advantages and disadvantages to each one as well as which one provides the best learning environment to your child.

	ADVANTAGES	DISADVANTAGES
Public		
Private		
Charter		
Home School		

CHAPTER 4

THE GLASS IS ALWAYS HALF FULL

———— ★ ————

Every day across this country, people, from corporate giants to stay-at-home moms realize the need to cultivate a positive attitude. We are often overwhelmed by the amount of pressure, deadlines and everyday responsibilities placed upon us. This can make keeping an optimistic point of view difficult at times and we must first look at what is necessary to maintain our own positive attitude before we can impact our children's. Our presence makes a difference. The future of our children requires us as parents to improve ourselves through an ongoing willingness to cultivate a positive attitude, make a recommitment to self-education and engage in small action steps to improve not only ourselves but our children as well.

Any parent can accomplish this and raise a terrific child. All that's needed is a desire to change our attitudes and implement constructive discipline. Parenting is at times difficult, and each one of us goes through phases when, regardless of our best efforts, we still find ourselves dealing with frustrating behaviors.

To deal with these types of situations some parents fret and worry while others lose their tempers. Rather than suffer from anxiety or yell at our children, we need to teach them that there are consequences for their behaviors. For instance, if they come home past curfew, they lose the privilege of going out the next week. If they get a speeding ticket, they not only can't drive for a week, but they also have to pay for the ticket and take a defensive driving course.

There are several factors such as your approach, methods, attitude and views that contribute to a child's behavior. First of all, you need to examine your own behavior when your child starts crying, throwing a temper tantrum or, in the case of teenagers, staying out all night or experimenting with drugs and alcohol. The approach you take determines whether or not they continue with their problem behavior. Rewarding them or ignoring the behavior only encourages them to act in the same manner.

BACK TO BASICS

I believe in traditional discipline and think that, while some positive reinforcement is good, the current trend of parents rewarding their children for every little thing has been a detriment to our children and society in general. Children need to learn that life doesn't reward every behavior, and they are going to lose sometimes. Parents have to have tough love and need to get back to basic values and making children responsible for their own behavior. My parents believed in a good spanking, although not abuse. When I was disciplined I learned a lesson and didn't repeat my mistakes. I wasn't harmed because I was spanked. In fact, I am a successful business owner and many of the values I have today I attribute to the way my parents raised me. I believe everyone will agree that they want the best for their children. To provide this, we need to stick to the method of discipline that is most effective.

One undeniable fact regardless of your parenting style is that children who are not properly disciplined are generally unhappy and unsuccessful. This is evident in our school systems today. Schools try to promote self esteem but there is little or no discipline. When discipline is used the rules are so vague that it is often applied inconsistently. When children are given no boundaries, they feel lost. If they have been given boundaries, on the other hand, they understand the concept of negative consequences and respect for authority. My children understand the concept of consequences: when they do something bad there's a negative consequence and when they do well there's a positive consequence.

Children need to learn lessons that are going to help them in the future. For instance, there are natural consequences for every action. If they don't study they are going to fail and if they don't practice they're not going to win. Positive reinforcement regardless of performance robs our children of real feedback. All of this fluff parenting (as I like to call it) glosses over the real issues and robs parents of the opportunity to engage in teachable moments. Drugs and sexual activity are on the rise. Parents seem to be afraid of hurting their children's feelings or taking away their rights. In my opinion children have few rights when their safety is at stake and emotions and feelings take a back seat to values. Children need real feedback instead of falsely-created "positivity" that ignores the real issues. Avoiding reality in this way actually encourages more disciplinary acts.

YOU DON'T HAVE TO YELL

One misconception about old school discipline is that it involves yelling and spanking. You don't have to do either if you remain calm and under control. Our children are constantly learning. They're like sponges, absorbing every little drop you place in front of them, which is why it is so important to keep our composure as parents. We have to be careful to not ignore or reward them for behavior we don't like, and instead reintroduce the behavior we do like. When everything is going along well, when we are on a roll, kids are learning and everyone seems content. It feels good, doesn't it - to be in this positive flow? You feel much more relaxed and you are enjoying your quality time with your kids. When something negative comes along it can be far more challenging for us to choose the positive path. So what do you do?

If negative situations appear, you don't have to scream and get angry. When we act this way, we're teaching our children to do the same. Instead, stay calm and learn to handle conflict in a constructive manner. Don't fight your negative feelings, acknowledge and accept them, then decide that you will choose to feel the positive emotions rather than the negative. I believe we can teach our children how to effectively voice their complaints in a respectful way that would serve them well.

Below is a copy of the original letter I sent to US Airways. I wrote this letter in response to a negative travel experience in hope that it would serve as a model on how to calmly express the anger felt by our family.

Dear Mr. Parker:

We have been US Airways frequent flyers for many years and have always been delighted to fly with you. Our loyalty has been shaken, however, by a recent frightening and potentially dangerous experience involving our eight year old daughter Kaitlyn.

On November 25, 2007 we were traveling with our family. We were confirmed on US Airways Flight 363 departing Phoenix in route to Sacramento. We had used Web Check in to obtain our boarding passes but were unable to select seats during the check in process. We arrived at the airport two hours in advance of our flight's scheduled departure but discovered that our reservation agent double booked the flight's seats.

Volunteers were sought but, because of the holiday weekend, the airline was unable to locate or confirm seats on any airline that day, no one was willing to be rebooked without a confirmed reservation. Despite our protests, we were informed that there was no room for us on the flight. At the very last minute we were told that three seats were available and that if 3people in the party would like to travel on flight 363 they would have to board immediately; the remainder of the party would be put on the next available flight. My husband boarded the flight accompanied by our fifteen year old son and eight year old daughter.

My older son and I were working with the gate supervisor, Eric to locate a flight. We were told that there was not a single seat available on any flight to Sacramento and the very first flight available was on Monday, the next day. As we stood at the desk watching the plane pull away my daughter suddenly appeared at my side, tears running down her cheeks. She said that the flight attendant told her that there weren't any more seats and that she would have to get off the plane. The attendant told her to go back outside. Kaitlyn said she told the attendant that her dad was on the plane but, she made her get off anyway. Kaitlyn was not walked back to my custody nor was her father told that she had been removed from the plane.

As I calmed Kaitlyn, I asked my son to call his dad on the cell phone and leave a message to let him know that Kaitlyn was with us and safe. I also asked the supervisor, Eric to call the plane to get a message to my husband. The supervisor made the call; however, he showed no outward sign of concern for my child or urgency. The three of us were offered compensation for our missed flight and confirmed on another flight on November 26, 2007.

I called the customer service line only to receive a pre-recorded message saying that due to the high volume of calls there would be no one available to talk with and to please go online to log a complaint. I did go online and read your Customer Promise of safety and satisfaction as well as your Customer Service Plan. I feel that you fell short of the mark in every area; double booking the flight, separating our family and endangering and upsetting our eight year old daughter by removing her from the plane without informing my husband and without checking to see if we were still at the gate.

The last time Rick saw his daughter, a female flight attendant told him that they could not sit together but, she would seat Kaitlyn up front and take care of her. After the plane was moving, Rick was told that one of his two kids was deplaned; the male flight attendant that spoke with Rick did not know which one. Rick was not allowed to get out of his seat for almost twenty minutes after takeoff during which time he, as any parent would be, was panicked. More than two hours passed before he was able to confirm the whereabouts and safety of his daughter.

I paid in advance to confirm my reservation. Moreover, we had a contract and a promise of safety. You had an obligation to reserve and hold my seat. You also had an obligation to ensure the safety of my family. I feel strongly that the flight attendant who made the decision to deplane my daughter should be fired and gate personnel who exercised extremely poor judgment should be sanctioned and required to complete a safety training program so that this sort of incident will not be repeated.

Nothing can compensate my family for the emotional trauma it sustained, but I want to ensure that you think seriously about your commitment to your customers. Ultimately, treating them badly will only bring you bad publicity and loss of business.

Please call me to confirm that disciplinary action was taken against those employees involved and to confirm that we, as a family, will be compensated for this distressing experience. I have already filed a report with the Flyers Rights Hotline and if l do not hear from you, I will report US Airways to the appropriate regulatory agencies in Arizona and California.

Sincerely,
Leslie Youra

cc: Vice President of Customer Service East Ross Banano

The airline chose to treat the incident as a non-event and both the letter I sent and my calls went unanswered until I engaged in what I would call a media stampede. An interview, article, news story, political rally or prime time special came out every month for almost a year following the incident. Only after the Dateline interview and a Travel Channel Special did they take it upon themselves to call and offer an apology.

During this time life went on as normal at home. We never discussed the incident in negative terms; instead, we talked about what a genuine blessing it was the situation turned out as it did, with everyone safe and sound in the end. It was important for Rick and me that our children understood that there is a right way and a wrong way to voice dissatisfaction with the system and that even when you are complaining or challenging the status quo you can do it with dignity and respect.

This story is important and connects very strongly to Kyle's experience at school because he was advised not to make waves. I believe in respecting those in authority. However I do not believe our children should be taught to ignore their intuition nor taught that it is wrong to speak out; it is not only a First Amendment right, but our duty to ourselves to speak up. Unfortunately, children and even parents do not always have role models to guide them through the process.

It takes determination, strength, faith, and the power of your will to focus on the positive when intense negativity descends. As you learn to focus on the positive, think positively, speak positively and take positive actions. Your children will soon follow. Suddenly you will look around you and you will find that the negativity has gone, and that strife and frustration have been replaced by tranquility and joy.

LET GO OF THE NEGATIVE

Take the time to learn this skill and you will see that in time you can easily let go of the negative emotions in your life and fill your mind with only positive, constructive emotions. This mindset is profoundly important in maintaining a positive environment in the home. I truly believe that building on positives is 80 percent mindset. The other 20 percent depends on your skills as a parent. We need to teach our children to have a positive attitude. This optimism, learned at an early age, is part of what makes children resilient. Resilient people bounce back from the setbacks of life. Developing this resilience is crucial in that it helps kids to:

★ notice and control their own emotions

★ develop and maintain a good sense of self-esteem

★ believe in their ability to make a difference to their lives and to achieve what they set out to achieve

Resilient kids can recognize their strengths and talents and accept their failures and setbacks. They feel a need for and are able to build and maintain good relationships with others.

Many parents don't believe they can change. The truth is anyone can learn to think positively and teach children to do the same if they are willing to change. You can learn to think optimistically and as a result you can teach your children to think positively as well. In a world of negativity and pressure, our children need to have hope. Our children are bombarded with negativity from the media in addition to facing increasing pressures daily from their peers, school and society as a whole which has a detrimental effect on their mental and physical health, academic and work success, and overall happiness.

Help them to look at the situation with hope rather than fear. They can think that they're not smart and going to flunk or they can ask themselves, "Where do I have control? What can

I do to make this situation better? What can I learn from this struggle?" and then take the necessary steps to improve their grades. Because positive children focus on what they can do to regain control of a situation, they don't slip into helplessness. And because they persist, they tend to succeed.

When children believe in themselves and gain confidence, they can accomplish whatever they put their minds to. As parents, we can teach children of all ages how to think positively and how to approach problems and adversities with a clear set of coping skills. This will enable them to approach their lives with resilience and persistence as well as increase their overall sense of well-being. Positive parenting, rather than "positive reinforcement", is the best method to raise our children, because only then can they inherit optimistic thinking by the example you set. Children always look up to and learn from their parents. Positive parents raise positive kids. When we begin to understand this, we set an outstanding example for them and ultimately it influences their friends, their choices, their actions and their lives. What more could any parent want?

★

EXERCISE

What are some areas that you and your child need to be more positive in? Make a list and then write down some actions the two of you can take to turn a negative into a positive.

CREATING A POSITIVE ATTITUDE

Parent	Child

Actions	Actions

CHAPTER 5

DREAMS REALLY
DO COME TRUE

───────── ★ ─────────

How many of our children and young adults are living their lives according to what society expects of them? Children today aren't taught to dream. Society's message is that we are to study hard, work hard, be responsible, get a good steady job, make more money, climb the corporate ladder and retire. That's what our parents did and they expected us to do the same, so as a result many parents expect the same of their children. This message is heard throughout our lives and has a dramatic impact on our young people. Most of them believe they have no choice but to follow the expectations set for them.

People who accomplish big feats in life always dream big. I am an avid believer in the phrase, "follow your dreams". I repeat this slogan every morning as a good reminder to myself to continue believing in myself and striving to become a success in my business ventures. One of the primary lessons I want my children to learn is to dream and realize that it doesn't have to remain a dream. I don't want them stuck in a job they can't stand and one day look back on their life with regret. As Walt Disney said, "All your dreams can come true if you have the courage to pursue them". These are wise words from a visionary genius who made a success out of dreaming.

We have to teach and encourage our children to dare to dream and then pursue their vision with all their heart, believing that it is truly achievable. Many times people don't tell others what their dreams are because they're afraid of rejection and ridicule. Each one of us has met a person who told us that our dreams were ridiculous or impossible. Our children are discouraged from daydreaming in school; they're told to focus and pay attention. Obviously focus is important, but dreams are valuable, too. If I asked you want you wanted most for your children, most of you would answer that you wanted them to be happy. One of the main ways to find fulfillment is learn about all that life has to offer. Our children are going to learn from us. If for no other reason than our love for our children, we need to teach them to dream.

Life is a journey and our dreams are wonderful preludes to what the future holds. Albert Einstein did his best thinking while dreaming. As a matter of fact when he was a student, his teachers considered him too much of a dreamer to ever be a success. He worked for several years as a clerk in the Swiss Patent Office, which allowed him the freedom to spend several hours a day staring out of the window in contemplation, which eventually gave birth to the Theory of Relativity. Let us learn from Einstein and don't be afraid to dream and expand our horizons. The only thing that can stop us from following our dreams and succeeding is ourselves.

FOLLOW YOUR DREAMS

How many times have you heard a successful person say that they are where they are today because they did what they loved and dreamed of doing? They had the courage to follow their dreams. Oftentimes people are very confused about what it means to do this. So first of all, let's look at what a dream actually is. The word dream, in this context, refers to our inner yearning or deepest desire. Our dreams are what lie deep within our core. They are what we want more than anything. As parents, we sometimes want our children to follow our dreams rather than theirs. We have to let go and allow them to have their own dreams.

When my husband was young he dreamed of being a farmer but his family talked him out of it, saying, "There's no money in farming". Later, when he had the opportunity to buy his first house and own a business, his former spouse listed all of the reasons that they couldn't afford to do either. But he knew in his heart and soul that he could make it happen if he just set his mind to the task. What did he do? He took action and the pieces began to fall in to place as if someone was supernaturally guiding them.

While it is important to support others' dreams and goals, whether it be a spouse, a child or a friend, you cannot live for their dreams nor can you expect them to live for yours. Each of us must live our own lives, clarify our dreams, and find where our passions lie. Your children's dreams are authentic passions that emanate from the essence of their being. It is not the role their moms, dads, grandparents, teachers or friends to develop or expect anything from them.

We have to be careful however, to make sure we encourage dreams, not fantasies. The difference between the two is that a dream is a "calling" while a fantasy is more "me" centered and materialistic. Fantasies are usually based on what we've been taught to believe is important such as making lots of money or becoming famous. For example, if your child says she wants to be a rock star, let her explore music or singing. If you see that she doesn't have the motivation to learn and work at it, she's probably chasing a fantasy rather than fulfilling a dream.

Since we live in a society that promotes and glamorizes materialism we need to be cautious about what we encourage our children to do. Spend some time with your children and talk to them to help determine the source of their motivation —is it authentic or superficial? We need to teach our children to decipher what they truly want (their dream) as opposed to what is expected of them. To do this, we first need to encourage them to stop looking to the outside for happiness. They don't need validation from friends or anyone else to make them happy. Their focus has to shift from thinking that they must get something—such as money, friends, car, looks, fame or anything else—to be content.

Our children all have unique talents, but the key is that they have to act on them. My mother used to tell me that if we don't use our God-given talents, He'll take them away and give them to someone who will put them to good use. We all have gifts and talents, but we must acknowledge them, "open" them and be willing to share them with the world. When you use them, they grow to serve you even better. It's not enough to be talented. All children have potential. However unless they act on it, potential is all they have. Dreams don't magically come true. Action is required. My husband and I tell our children all the time that they have super potential in one area or another and then we take a step further and help them look for ways to grow and expand.

Your dreams are an important part of your growth. My friend's son didn't know what he wanted to study after high school. His main hobby was working on cars but he didn't know if that was to be his profession. He started business school and dragged his feet every day, hardly able to get to classes in time. He had neither interest nor enthusiasm for the classes, and he continued to work on cars as often as he could. He decided to quit business school and started to work for a car company. It was long hours starting early in the morning, but he was a new kid after he made this change. He jumped out of bed each day, worked hard and was fantastic in his job, resulting in promotions and increased responsibilities. His life was fulfilled because he had the courage to follow his dreams.

As soon as your children are old enough to dream, encourage them to do so. It is also important to teach children that following their dreams doesn't mean that they'll always love what they are doing every given moment. There are going to be times when they'll have to do certain things that they don't want to do in order to fulfill their dreams. Hard work and unexpected setbacks are ingredients to any dream, but with perseverance, your children will experience an overall sense of direction, purpose and fulfillment. In addition to work and setbacks, children need to learn to accept the tradeoffs involved in living their dream. Life gives us no guarantees. If, for instance, your child dreams of being a concert pianist and they show talent and are willing to act on their potential, one of the consequences may be trading time with friends for practice time. These lessons are vital if we want our children to be successful, happy adults.

In this as in other things, it is vitally important for you to live the lessons that you want to impart to your kids. Take a look at your life right now. Are you excited and alive in what you are doing or is what you are doing leaving you feeling drained and depleted? What type of example are you setting for your children?

BELIEVING IS SEEING

Everything in this world is created twice, first in the mind and then in reality. Your results will always reflect your expectations. Many people want a better life, a new exciting job, but they never expect it to happen. Instead they say to themselves: "These things never happen to me, it's just a silly dream." If you want it but don't expect it, it's wishful thinking.

In order for you to expect greatness in your life you must learn to visualize it so that you can take action. Athletes are a good example. They create clear pictures in their minds and expect to win. In fact, they often visualize their entire competition in their minds before the contest even begins. They know how they will respond to challenges so when those challenges come, they are prepared, like Les Brown was prepared when he got his opportunity to take over a radio program. He was ready and because of it, he won!

Visualization is the picturing power of your mind. We are constantly running a mental movie with ourselves as star of the show. When we use the power of visualization we bring ourselves closer to the success we desire. Visualization and dreams are tightly linked because they both engage our emotions through imagination. One of the reasons visualization is so effective is because our mind and body don't really know the difference between what we imagine and reality. When we imagine scenarios in their lives, our bodies and minds react as if they were true.

I need to point out however that believing something to be true doesn't guarantee that it will happen. Our children can believe and visualize that they're going to make an A on their history test or get a job right out of high school making $70,000 va year, but without action it isn't going to happen. We have to teach them to take deliberate action steps as well as dream and visualize.

For many children and teenagers, taking action is difficult due to lack of confidence or lack of belief in themselves. Visualization, because it taps directly into these emotions, can strengthen our belief in ourselves and our goals. When we're just beginning to use visualization we begin by simply seeing what is happening in our imagination. It isn't until we add our five senses that we truly enhance the experience and amplify our results. Sight, touch, smell, taste, and hearing can all be integrated into your visualizations.

In the case of a sixteen year old boy, for instance, one of his biggest dreams may be to get a car. In our family, there was no new car sitting in the driveway with a bow on it. Our children had to work and earn the money to pay for their cars. Along with finding a job, we taught them to visualize their car and hear to the radio, feel the steering wheel and to use their other senses as well. They loved this exercise and it motivated them to work harder toward their goal.

When we teach our children to visualize, we were actually giving them permission to daydream. What child doesn't like to do that! The better they become at visualization and the more willing they are to take deliberate action the sooner they'll accomplish their dreams.

Make visualization a family affair and look for situations where you can visualize together. Imagine your family succeeding at a longstanding goal. Maybe you want to take a cruise or move into the family dream home. Like anything else it takes practice. Visualization is a powerful concept because when we visualize our success as reality we can also visualize the path to get there. What steps are you taking? What is working for you? How do you feel and what can you do to reach success?

GOALS

One of the best methods to teach your children to prepare for the future is to set goals. So many of our children don't have a plan or a clear vision of what they want in life. When the entire family is involved in the goal setting process, it focuses more energy on achieving the intended goal. The best method to reach a goal is to see the end in mind and work your way backwards. We all have dreams and each of us has set goals at one time or another which have helped us accomplish great things, whether that meant buying our first car, getting a new job or promotion, meeting that special person or buying a house. However often we are not aware that we are setting goals for ourselves. When our dreams are big enough and we can see ourselves in possession of that dream our mind naturally helps us set goals and develop a plan. Review your own life. What are three things that you have accomplished?

Looking back on my own life with a heightened sense of awareness, I find that I have always been a dreamer, a goal setter and a doer and because of this I have attained much. Some goals I set were given greater priority yet were slow to materialize, while others were attained quickly and with relative ease. In each case it was action that helped me to realize my goal. It is also important to point out that not every dream or goal has come to pass exactly as I imagined.

Goal setting is a crucial skill we have to pass on to our children for them to succeed. The process of goal setting allows them to create a plan for where they want to go in life. In order for them to achieve their life's dreams, they must first concentrate their efforts on a strategic plan. With each goal our children effectively set and achieve, they'll begin to develop more self confidence. Success brings greater success.

As with visualization, goal setting is used by successful people in all walks of life. Paint a vivid picture in your mind of what you want and then confidently take the steps needed to move forward. With the crystal-clear picture of your goal in mind, visualize your arrival. A mistake that I see so many parents make when they set goals is to base them on what they know they can achieve. When you do this, you are teaching your children to settle for safe, mediocre results.

There is no inspiration in goals that are well within your comfort zone. In most of the jobs we have today we're expected to set goals in this manner. For instance, I know that many companies base their future growth on last year's results. Rick and I have made it a point not set goals for our business on past accomplishments. In order to stretch and grow you must have a goal that excites you and scares you, too. You and must be inspired to stretch and find new ways of reaching it. You must use your imagination when deciding on your goals. Start with what you truly want, without placing restrictions on your vision. What do you really want to achieve? Go for the investments of time that stretch your abilities and require a high level of creativity and energy to conquer.

Our children need to learn that life has bumps and they'll never learn to achieve their dreams if they quit at each obstacle. In order to achieve success, and the life of your dreams, you have to see yourself accomplishing your goals and living how you would live once your goals have been reached. Your goals should create a burning desire deep within you. If you don't truly desire something, it is easy to become distracted and fail to follow through. So, it makes sense that your first step is have a goal that you really want and to imagine the feelings you will have once the goal has been achieved. The stronger the feelings, the more motivated you will be, and the more quickly your goals will be manifested.

When we teach our children—teenagers in particular—to set effective goals, we must make sure to tell them to:

★ Make positive statements. When you talk about your goals use positive expressions. Use phrases like, 'I can do this,' instead of 'Don't be stupid and mess up."

★ Give your goals precise dates, times, and amounts so you can measure your achievements and success.

★ Prioritize your goals. Give each of your goals a priority. This practice helps you to avoid feeling overwhelmed by too many goals, and helps to direct your attention to the most important ones.

★ Write all of your goals down. This will help to reinforce them in your mind. Review this list often and place it anywhere that you will see it each day.

★ Keep your goals on a realistic time frame. If a goal has an unrealistic time frame it can seem that you are not making progress toward it. Setting goals with realistic time frames gives more opportunities for reward.

★ Stack your goals. Today's goals should be derived from larger goals.

One of the techniques we've taught our children is to make a list of all of their goals. It does not matter how ridiculous or impossible the ideas seem--just write them down. When their list is complete, we review it with them and talk about the one that really excites them. It is critical that you spend time visualizing yourself achieving your goal, which is why I encourage our children to make goal cards. A goal card is nothing more than a piece of paper you carry around with your goals written on it.

I carry around my goals on a goal card and read them several times a day, creating constant pictures in my mind. If you can't picture your goals, then you probably won't achieve them. Focus on your goals and ask yourself these questions:

★ What do I have to do each day to achieve my goals?

★ Am I willing to take responsibility to accomplish these tasks?

After your children have achieved a goal, take a moment to celebrate their accomplishment. Talk with them about how this has furthered their progress toward other goals and explore any additional actions they need to accomplish them. I believe that you can use many different strategies to set your goals and the most powerful of these strategies is to dream. If you're going to dream, dream big, as big as you can, because by dreaming you will force your subconscious mind into action. Create a vivid picture in your mind--one that ignites your passion and fills your senses. Have fun, be enthusiastic and remember that it is your life and this is your dream.

My children have specific goals, well-defined plans and have taken massive action. They have always done something. They are doers. Keep this in mind when teaching your children to set their own goals. Pick goals for which you have tremendous passion and a strong desire. Don't worry about whether these goals are attainable or not, just go after them. There is no dream and no goal that is too big for you to accomplish.

How can you ignite your passion and stir the fire deep within your soul? What is it that brings joy to your life? When you are able to answer these questions, hold on to your passion and do not settle for anything less than your ideal. You will then have the life of your dreams. Remember that whatever your dreams are, that they are not actually going to happen unless you take the necessary actions and steps, and put in the hard work and effort to make them a reality. So why don't you get dreaming and figure out what you really desire out of life? Why settle for anything less? Another great quote from Walt Disney: "If you can dream it, you can do it." There is also Bible verse that I enjoy that says, "As a man thinks in his heart, so is he." There is absolute truth to that. We can accomplish almost anything we set our minds to.

━━━━━━━━━ ★ ━━━━━━━━

EXERCISE

On the next page write down your goals and then ask your children to do the same. After you've made your list of goals, create a goal card and then have your child do the same.

(PARENT) MY GOALS ARE...

_____

_____

_____

_____

_____

_____

_____

(CHILD) MY GOALS ARE...

_____

_____

_____

_____

_____

_____

_____

(Parent) Goals: Accomplish Date:

(Child) Goals: Accomplish Date:

CHAPTER 6

LET THERE BE PEACE

★

More than ever before, our country suffers from a lack of parental control. In the past, parents insisted on respect from their children and expected them to do what they were told. Now, it seems just the opposite. Parents today act as if they're scared of their children or they don't want to inhibit their creativity or break their spirit. Many cater to their children's every need without considering the consequences for either the child or themselves later in life. My oldest son moved out on his own a few months back. He didn't want to abide by our rules, so we gave him the option of doing what we say or finding another place to live. In fact, my husband told him that he had better hurry and move out while he knew everything. After he moved out into the real world, he suddenly realized that dishes don't just magically do themselves, clothes aren't self folding and people who you thought were your friends will disappoint or take advantage of you. Now, he is more appreciative of what he had. He has more understanding, love and respect for his parents, family and home.

Respect is the gateway to discipline. In this chapter, we'll discuss the need for respect as well as go into detail about one common error most of today's parents make—they want to be their children's friends. Once you cross this boundary your authority diminishes. The balance of power shifts and you are now an equal in the eyes of your child. Along with the lack of respect, once you become your children's friend there is a sense of entitlement that plagues them. Through a misguided sense of entitlement they lose sight of what it means to work hard and actually earn their way in this world. I believe that these three items are crucial for a well balanced child, which is why I've dedicated an entire chapter and an exercise at the end of this chapter to:

★ Respect

★ Being a parent not a friend

★ Entitlement

RESPECT

Some parents would rather let their children act like monsters to avoid hurting their feelings than rein them in to teach them respect and the value of discipline. While I was in education, I saw an alarming trend with my students. They lacked discipline. Most of the problems in school today are a direct result of no discipline at home. Recently, Rick and I watched a standup comedian talk about how he used to threaten to report his parents to Child Protective Services for child abuse if they made him do something he didn't want to do. One day his father called his bluff and told him, "Go ahead and report me. True, I may get into a little bit of trouble. But those people need exactly 30 minutes to get to our house and during those 30 minutes you're mine."

Times change, but the way in which we discipline our children shouldn't. Before parents became so concerned with "positive reinforcement" children learned the value of hard work, fairness, and respect. We didn't have little league games where score wasn't kept because we didn't want our children to lose. Instead we taught them that life isn't always easy and that competition is good. Our children need discipline. They may not readily agree with us, but we're the parents and it is our job to teach them about real life.

Discipline is effective. It lets our children know there are consequences for their actions whereas positive reinforcement rewards them for a job undone. Children that understand that there are consequences of misbehavior learn to be responsible and that there are absolutes in life. For instance, when I was a child, I remember playing with an old battery in the garage. My father told me to stop but I ignored him and received a spanking. Why? Not because he wanted to be mean and keep me from having a good time. Dad wanted to protect me from getting hurt because the battery was leaking acid. Rules aren't made to be broken. They're made to help us become better and more productive members of society and keep us safe.

For me, the primary driving force of discipline is respect for authority. During my childhood, parents truly had their children's respect and passed on knowledge to the younger generation. In these times of young princes and princesses, respect has been replaced with a sense of entitlement. Children don't care what their parents have to say anymore. They want to do as they please. Society has neglected the importance of inculcating the virtue of respect toward authority in our young ones and teenagers. As parents we shouldn't have to earn our children's respect, we should instead command it. There is no such thing as earned respect in the realm of parenting. v

I'M NOT YOUR FRIEND

When we "befriend" our children rather than parent them, we're doing them a huge disservice. Once you become their friend, you've lost all authority in their eyes. Moms and dads should be parents to their children, not friends, buddies or pals. There are consequences to being the "cool" mom or dad. You become an equal to them and they no longer feel the need to listen to you. A recent ad campaign that ran across the country showed a picture of teens telling their parents to help them stay sober and stop buying alcohol for them. How far have our values as parents fallen when we have to advertise correct behavior? When we take responsibility and act as parents not pals we reduce the risk of our children smoking, drinking, using drugs and having sex.

Friends don't discipline, they don't teach, instead they go along with one another, which puts parents in an impossible position when it comes to enforce the rules of the house. Ask yourself this: if you are busy being your child's best friend, who is acting as the parent in their lives? A lifestyle for a happy childhood requires routines and time with family and friends of an appropriate age. Parents who view their children as their friends can give them a false sense of place and a confusion of role boundaries. In an ideal family life, clear boundaries are set for children so that they know who the adults are, what their roles are and learn to respect those adults.

Many parents attempt to become their children's friends in a desperate plea to stay connected. In reality, they almost always lose touch with their children. Children need consistency and stability. If one day you're letting them slide on their chores and the next day you're telling them to be home by curfew you're confusing them. They need to know without doubt that they can predict consequences from their parents in response to their actions. They need discipline they can count on and to know that if they make a mistake their parents will be there to listen, not solve their problems for them. Children with strong parents who are willing to discipline them learn independence and build self esteem.

Responsible parents wouldn't prevent their children from eating or let them go to school naked. The same is true about giving them independence, confidence and self esteem. We need to stop preventing them from gaining the skills they need to have in society. They don't need you as a friend; they have plenty from school and church. Our goal as parents is to give them the tools to set and achieve goals and become successful in their own right.

In *Awaken the Giant Within*, Anthony Robbins talks about the need we, as humans, have to avoid pain and move toward pleasure. This is instinctive in humans. Otherwise, why obey? "Go to your room." "No." "Give me your keys, you're grounded." "No!" Why should our children do as they are told unless, at some point, a little unpleasant consequence is administered? Of course, there are those who disagree and think that we should just reason with our children and if we resort to such a violent tactic as a swat on the rear we are bad parents and our parenting style is archaic. However reason does not always prevail because our children are still learning their reasoning skills, and they cannot accomplish this difficult task without a structured and well-ordered routine. Parental discipline is a substitute for self-discipline while children are in their formative years. When I was young, if I misbehaved I was spanked. After the first few swats, I learned to behave correctly to avoid a spanking. Such is the simplicity and effectiveness of conscientious punishment.

Now let me make one point clear, before I go any further. I believe we should use spankings for effectiveness and not to hurt the child. I agree that kids shouldn't be "beaten", of course, but there's nothing wrong with a swat on the behind when they're acting up. My grandfather used to say, "take care of it now while they're young or you'll be bailing them out of jail when they're sixteen." When children get out of control, the police aren't going to use positive reinforcement or spare their feelings. They're just going to throw them in jail.

Disrespect is a major problem faced by parents. For some reason children sometimes believe they have the right to dictate terms to their parents. The situation has to be dealt with immediately. It is necessary for the parents to realize that rather than always being friendly or joking around, they sometimes need to be forceful with their child. Irritation and anger won't help the situation, so stay calm and composed and don't indulge in any kind of screaming match. If they speak to you in an inappropriate manner, ignore them. Immediately stop talking and decline to answer if they ask you something. Instead tell them that you're ready only when they learn to behave and act appropriately.

Also, don't pacify your child. They don't need a slew of choices as to how to behave or speak to you. They only need one—do what you say. Draw the line. If you do not approve of any of your child's behavior, tell them straight away that you expect them to act accordingly. Let them know what is expected and what is unacceptable. You, not your child, set the limits for their behavior and conduct in the house.

Touchy feely parenting has produced a certain kind of adult: those who think they can do as they please without ever having to answer for their behavior. Everyone I knew growing up in the 60s and 70s received some form of corporal punishment if they misbehaved. Where children are concerned, some sort of physical discipline has to be an option, if only as a back up to reinforce other forms of discipline. A study conducted by psychology professor Marjorie Gunnoe at Calvin College in

Grand Rapids, Michigan, reported that children spanked up to the age of 6 were likely as teenagers to perform better at school and were more likely to carry out volunteer work and to want to go to college than their peers who had never been physically disciplined. I totally agree with these findings.

Our children need to realize that there are consequences for their behaviors. I was spanked as a child and I'm not angry, aggressive or violent. I don't have low self esteem or lack of confidence. I do however have the ability to think for myself and the drive to succeed, much of which I attribute to the way my parents disciplined me. They taught me that I had to be responsible and didn't let me get away with misbehavior.

When I was spanked, my parents always let me know the reason for the punishment. For instance, one time as a little girl I ran into the street after my ball. My mother saw me, ran to the front and said, "I told you not to go out in the street because you could get hit by a car, but you did it anyway, so you're getting a spanking." Also, the spanking wasn't a "beating" as so many people believe spankings are. It was just enough to make me realize I didn't want to get another one. Marjorie Gunnoe's study is a welcome relief in the world of "parenting experts" who accentuate the detriments of spanking, which have been used to justify anti-spanking laws in some areas of our country. Our government doesn't have the right to tell us how to discipline our children.

To some parents, discipline is a dirty word. They tend to be overly permissive, set poor examples, be inconsistent with boundaries and not teach responsibility. I can't believe that so many parents don't view themselves as absolute authority figures, instead treat their family as a democracy, and trying to be friends rather than parents to their children.

A SENSE OF ENTITLEMENT

One of the most difficult attitude problems the workforce faces today is the younger generation's sense of entitlement. So many young adults think they deserve a high paying job just because they're college graduates, or worse that some jobs are beneath them because they have a diploma. Even with my kids, I see some entitlement. They expect me to help them with homework or do their laundry. It's natural to feel entitled, especially for teenagers, which is why it is so important to make our children realize they are not entitled to anything on this planet. This may sound harsh, but it is the truth.

Our culture fosters these notions in us. For instance, when the government bailed out the banks they sent a message that if you get into trouble someone's going to take care of you. Our children are growing up more and more with a strong sense of entitlement today. Parents and schools reward them each day for small tasks that should be expected. A child should never be rewarded for chores or good grades. In my day, I was expected to make A's and keep my room clean.

Sometimes parents don't want to enter into a conflict because it is just easier to let their children do what they want. It may be easy now, but when they're living in your basement or garage at 40, you'll wish you had made different decisions when they were younger. Some parents don't want to say "no" because they're afraid their children won't like them. Parenting isn't always the easiest endeavor or the most popular. There are many popular parents with children in prison or rehab. The choice is yours.

Children learn more from us than we realize. The old adage that actions speak louder than words is true when it comes to children. Many children feel a sense of entitlement in life because they have been taught to do so by their parents. From birth children learn to react according to their environment. We need to watch our behaviors. Are we teaching our children a sense of entitlement? How many times do you dig into your wallet or purse every time your child asks for money? Do you make them earn their money or fork it over at their convenience? Stop and think about the message you send them each time you give them money without the expectation of receiving something of value in return. If you don't expect your children to contribute to their own daily care or the upkeep of the house they don't develop the skill of creating their own future. Teaching them responsibility also teaches them goal-setting, self worth, and independence.

In our home, we have a set of chores and responsibilities for our children. They make their own beds, clean up after themselves, do their laundry, and when we're working late, cook their own meals. Hard work is the best technique we have to teach them the value of earning something for themselves. If parents give their children responsibilities they won't grow up feeling they are more important than anyone else. Our parenting philosophy is that we want our children to know how much we love them, but they need to realize that not everyone is going to agree with how we feel. We want to develop a character in them that they will learn to build upon as they mature and meet new people in life. We're teaching our children to earn the respect of others rather than expect it.

So do your children a favor and give them a set of chores and responsibilities, then hold firm even when they challenge you. When we cater to the every whim of our children we create a feeling that the world owes them. When our children feel entitled, they focus on what they are owed, not what they might need to give to others. It is a "one-way street" mind-set. Then once they go out into the real world and people don't meet their expectations, they find themselves confused, resentful, and angry because the rest of the world doesn't give them whatever they want. They're shocked that they actually have to work for something. To me, giving your child a false sense of entitlement is a much worse form of child abuse than spanking.

Rather than give your children a sense of entitlement, instead give them the self assurance needed to find and follow their own happiness and dreams without depending on anyone else to do it for them. Teach your children to set goals and achieve them, and when they finally do so they'll realize how good it feels to do it on their own. Once they experience the feeling of earning something on their own versus having it handed to them, they'll learn a new sense of appreciation and respect for what they have.

It is time to stop raising entitled children. When they learn to think for themselves and develop confidence to find their own way, our job as a parent is more rewarding. Children learn what they live in a more intense way than they ever do through what they are told. They watch and emulate us. When they are told they should act a certain way they hardly hear it at all. When they see us behave responsibly, show respect and work hard, they hold onto a little bit of that wisdom for themselves. Be responsible, be a parent, but most of all set a good example for your children.

We can't be too soft on our children. If we don't teach them respect through discipline someone else will. People who don't respect their parents aren't going to respect anyone else. Our children are not little princes or princesses; they are no better than we were at their age. One of my favorite quotes is "What doesn't kill you makes you stronger" and sweeping the floor, mowing the grass and washing dishes isn't going to kill our children. So parents: be careful you are not teaching your children to feel entitled, and most of all remember you're not their friend, you're their parent. We can still enjoy our children and have fun with them but they should always know the boundaries.

Loving our children doesn't mean either using brutally harsh punishment or showering them with gifts and cash. Loving our children means preparing them for the real world because we won't always be here to take care of them. When we create an environment of stability through discipline and respect, we develop a closer, more meaningful relationship with our children.

EXERCISE

In the space below make a list of chores for your children to do each day.

CHORES

1.

2.

3.

4.

5.

6.

7.

8.

9.

10.

CHAPTER 7

DOLLARS AND SENSE

★

Many of life's problems stem from money issues of one sort or another. So why is it that the discussion of financial issues in high school and college is often relegated to the margins, glossed over or neglected altogether? The answer is simple: because nobody likes to talk about it. Why is it difficult to discuss money and financial issues? Money and finances have deep meanings for people, meanings that go to deep layers of their psyches. For example, many consider money to be an extremely private issue that they are unwilling to share with one another. Friends may discuss stock investments but never their personal finances, incomes and overall wealth. Money relates directly to issues of high or low self-esteem, feelings of success or failure, power or weakness and what some may judge to be an individual's social conscience or economic exploitation of others. Money also relates to self-perceived feelings of dependence or independence.

Today an increasingly higher percentage of young people and teenagers is entering the real world with at least some debt. Far fewer have a plan for how to deal with the situation or an understanding of the negative effects the unacknowledged presence of debt can have on their lives. My son is a good example. He received a credit card and before he knew it he was five thousand dollars in debt. It is difficult to be frugal when it seems that our entire society is pushing people to spend money. The mass media, including such things as television, magazines, newspapers, the internet, etc. encourage people to purchase the latest in technology, such as HDTV, IPods, cellular phones and so on. In fact people are told that they can save money by making these purchases. If there ever were a paradox and conundrum for people this is it: this notion that they can save money by spending it!

Young people, like adults, can be overwhelmed by monthly bills that often exceed their monthly income. Filled with anxiety and anger, many don't know what to do or where to turn for help. It is a challenge for students to understand or face these issues, as they are mostly absent from discussion in school. Financial intelligence or competence is not a topic normally required or even included in teacher preparation or licensing. Teaching professionals often feel rushed, uncomfortable or ill-equipped to address this topic. Yet these avenues provide a tremendous opportunity for introducing new thoughts and approaches, to encourage communication about money management as cornerstones to becoming a productive member of society.

MONEY IS MORE THAN DOLLARS AND CENTS

Money is not only dollars and cents. It is also a symbol of personal attitudes toward life. With children, teenagers and young adults, the first essential step is to acquire financial attitudes that will harmonize with what they want out of life.

As a rule, happy people are successful not because they have no problems, but because they have learned how to face problems and arrive at working solutions.

You probably have noticed that different people have different attitudes about money. Some people want to collect as much as they can, while others want to buy as many goods and services as they can. We need to teach our children to strike a balance between these two extremes. These attitudes are developed early in life. For instance, a son's father and mother may have conflicting attitudes toward the importance and use of money. The following example illustrates different attitudes. A husband wants clothes and electronic equipment—the latest of everything, and believes that money is to be spent. When the money does not come along fast enough, he buys on credit. The wife on the other hand does not care about material things and thinks money is to be saved and invested. She likes to have a substantial bank account, investments and insurance. Her pleasure comes from watching the bank account grow.

Conflict is inevitable between these two people. He thinks she is stingy. She knows her husband is a spendthrift and is taking them right down the road to the poor house. What types of conflicting beliefs are instilled in their son when he witnesses these different types of attitudes toward money? Will his financial decisions in the future be made up of constant tension, worry, fear, ill feelings, arguments and bitterness?

Your attitudes about money are influenced by your environment and your past experiences. Consider a person who has lived through hard times when the family could not get enough to eat. That person's attitude toward money is different from that of a person who has always had enough or more than enough to satisfy their basic wants, as well as needs. Your values influence your financial choices. Economic security is greatly dependent upon the values and attitudes we hold regarding money. It is not how much money you have, but what you do with it and how you feel about it.

Basic physical needs are shelter, clothing and food. Wants are desires for more than the basics in life. Wants are often expressed in terms of material things like a DVD, a high definition LCD television or a swimming pool. Obviously some wants are closer to needs than the rest. What would be a frivolous want for one person might be a basic and satisfying want for another person. We need to develop and understand our attitudes toward money and decide what true personal or material value means to us in order to teach our children to do the same.

A Penny for Your Thoughts

You can't stick your head in the sand every time a financial issue arises. Both you and your children need to deal with the situation head on before it spirals out of control. Money is one of the greatest causes of arguments between parents and children, and living in a society where almost all of the financial messages that people receive are "spend, spend, spend," doesn't help an already-touchy subject.

Ideally, the best time to start discussing finances is before your child enters into the real world. Avoiding this discussion until afterwards can cause big problems later. As difficult as it may seem, discussing past money troubles, income disparities and financial obligation before your children move out can avoid major financial upheavals for them in the future. Also, exploring money styles and financial histories will help them create a money system that fits their needs.

If you're like most parents however, you don't worry about teaching your children about money while they are young. I strongly disagree! Start talking now. Don't wait until they are ready to move out on their own. Set time aside to have a frank conversation in which you talk to them about money management style, financial problems, tax liabilities, financial commitments, and retirement savings. Some questions you may answer to stimulate this conversation are:

★ When you make a purchase do you start saving for it, research it, shop around for the best deal or purchase it immediately?

★ Do you track your finances on a regular basis so you know the details of your financial situation at all times, periodically or not at all?

★ If you received money unexpectedly would you invest it, save it or spend it?

★ Do you pay your bills as soon as they arrive, when they are due, or when you get around to it? Do you spend what's left after the bills are paid or save it?

★ Do you pay your credit card balance in full each month, as much as you can or the minimum amount needed to maintain the account?

When it comes to teaching your children to manage money it is important to have regular money meetings to review how things are going with their finances. These meetings can help children stay on track and resolve problems before they become overwhelming. Money meetings should be at a specific time that is convenient for both of you, in a quiet place, and focus only on finances. You may want to set some ground rules to help the meeting go smoothly such as: talk about finances not people/each other, state concerns clearly without blame and if you become emotional during the meeting stop and either reschedule or take a break to calm down.

Each person states clearly how they see the problem. Once you're in a better frame of mind, take some time to brainstorm solutions. One person makes a list, all ideas are acceptable. Do not judge ideas as they are given. After you're finished making the list, review and evaluate the solutions, crossing out those that would not work for one or more reasons, accepting those ideas that are workable and agreeable to all involved. Now select one solution to work on first and outline steps needed to accomplish this solution. When you're making your outline be sure to identify problems that might arise and how you will deal with them. Also, allot some time to review the problem and see if you and your children are making progress.

WHAT'S MINE IS MINE AND WHAT'S YOURS IS MINE

Successful budgeting and money-handling doesn't magically happen just because we teach our children one or two financial lessons. It's something you have to keep working on as they grow. Start early and make it a habit to talk to your children about money. Every day there are dozens of little decisions to be made about money, such as whether or not to pay cash, write a check, use a credit card or pay a bill, not to mention the bigger decisions involving savings and investments, tax planning, ownership rights, insurance coverage and other matters with long-term consequences. Some of these may not seem important if your children are young, but time flies and before you know it you'll be watching them graduate high school and move out on their own.

Money equals power for many people and therefore control of finances, bank accounts, bills and how much you allow your child to spend implies who will and will not be in control. Older children and parents often begin to struggle with one another over these questions of finances. You may not realize that quite a few money problems stem from your emotions. Solving money difficulties requires both rational planning and insight. Over-indebtedness is one of the biggest money management problems teenagers and young adults face. Many over-indebted families have always been in debt which trickles down to the children's conceptions about money. As a result, these young people live on credit cards and consequently are continuously paying interest charges without eliminating any of the original debt.

Shared understandings around the use of money—who pays for what, when do I need to check in about a proposed purchase—need to be talked through early and often to avoid resentments and mistrust. Too often the conversations needed to develop common philosophy around spending and saving, giving and gifting, don't happen. Remaining stuck in family-of-origin patterns around finances, be they unhealthy hoarding or compulsive spending, can be damaging to children.

Many parents do not talk about money management with their children until there are problems. An already shaky financial future can get worse under the impact of money problems and heavy debts. Soon after some young people start out on their own, they may incur big debts because of too many purchases or commitments. Then they might be faced with a medical emergency, a cut in pay or unemployment. Up until the emergency occurred, the problem may not have been serious. However, as creditors press for payments and the budget tightens, problems begin.

Credit is useful if its potential role in family financing is understood and the credit is handled with its costs in mind. Unfortunately problems arise because "easy credit" is not easily rejected by people. A specific spending plan will help teenagers and young adults who want to solve their money problems. When devising a plan think about what you'll be spending the money on. What do you really need? Goal-setting is one of the first steps in a financial management program. Goals provide incentives for good management. One reason many people fail financially is because they have no long-term goals for which to strive. As a result, their lives and their incomes are frittered away.

Some financial goals are attainable immediately; some are attainable in the near future, while others are sought for a long period of time. Make your goals definite and attainable. Clearly-defined goals not only encourage the wise use of your resources, but also stimulate the cooperation of those who set the goals. In the early years of our marriage, we set up a number of goals as a blueprint for our future. The goals were written, framed and hung in the business center of the house. We always said, "Keeping the future in sight helps us do first things first, with an eye on the total scheme." We set the following goals:

★ Finish remodeling our home by the time our youngsters enter high school.

★ Save to help pay for the children's college educations.

★ Maintain a checking balance of at least $1000.

★ Open a savings account to be used for emergencies or unforeseen household repairs.

★ Contribute to worthwhile causes.

★ Plan a family vacation and set aside dollars to fund the trip.

★ Set aside a down payment in order to trade cars every 4 years.

★ Make money management a joint venture.

★ Agree on a realistic spending plan.

★ Adjust spending plan as circumstances change.

The fact that we knew what we wanted on a long-term basis, and what we needed to do to see our dreams come true, gave ourselves and our children a basis for making decisions and setting short-term goals. Review your goals from time to time, especially when major changes take place. Goals differ from one stage in our lives to another and from one individual to another so be prepared to discuss that with your children as well.

One of the most serious problems that can derail our financial goals is money management and credit card debt. Both parents and teenagers must learn how to handle their finances and this is no easy task. Money impinges on and can even threaten feelings about our autonomy and independence. Does money make us happy? Better yet, does having more money make us happier? We've probably all thought about these questions from time to time. Most of us have imagined what it would be like to trade places with someone rich and famous. We imagine a life where we could have almost anything we want, where people would recognize and appreciate us more, where we would be happier. It's understandable to think that having more money makes a person happier.

You might be surprised to know that research shows that people with more money are no happier than people with less money. Think about the wealthiest people you know or have heard of. Think of all the celebrities, athletic stars, and wealthy individuals who have gone through divorce, drug addiction and depression. Are these people really happier than the rest of us? Howard Hughes was one of the richest men the world had ever known yet he died alone, depressed, and terribly unhappy.

How important is money? No one can really answer that question for you. It's true that more money can make us more comfortable and make the everyday struggles of life easier to handle, but it does not necessarily affect core happiness. Money has an important place in our society. However, when asked to identify the keys to their happiness, most people put money far down the list. Here are some examples of other things that people commonly say are their "keys to happiness":

★ Good relationships with family

★ Strong friendships

★ Good health

★ Healthy marriage

★ Sense of accomplishment

★ Spirituality

★ Interesting activities

How about you? Where does money fit on your list? Test yourself. Look at the list above and pick one item that would be most important to your happiness. Add other items if you would like. Ask yourself these questions: "Would I like to be rich but in poor health?" "Would I like to drive a brand new car but have a terrible relationship with my children or parents?" Go through the rest of the list. What's really important to you? After you have picked the one item that is most important for your happiness, pick the second most important item. Keep going until you've listed all the items.

More money will not necessarily give you more happiness and contentment in life; but it can certainly help, provided you learn to manage it. This is an important lesson to pass on to your children.

★

EXERCISE

Marriages are partnerships and both parties have to be on the same page. Use the space below to make a list of both you and your spouse's financial goals. Remember, financial goal-setting is a continual process, and new goals should be formulated as situations change.

```
┌────────────────────────────────────────────────┐
│ OUR FINANCIAL GOALS ARE...                      │
│                                                  │
│                                                  │
│                                                  │
│                                                  │
│                                                  │
│                                                  │
│                                                  │
│                                                  │
└────────────────────────────────────────────────┘
```

Now sit down with your children and have them do the same.

```
┌────────────────────────────────────────────────┐
│ MY FINANCIAL GOALS ARE...                       │
│                                                  │
│                                                  │
│                                                  │
│                                                  │
│                                                  │
│                                                  │
│                                                  │
│                                                  │
└────────────────────────────────────────────────┘
```

CHAPTER 8

THE EXPANDING
CIRCLE OF
INFLUENCE

★

As parents, one of our primary responsibilities is to keep our children safe. We've helped them with each fall as they took their first steps and watched to make sure they made it in the door safely on their first day of school. But now that they're older, you may find yourself in unfamiliar territory. As they grow and demonstrate greater responsibility, they have the freedom to meet new friends, spend more time on the Internet, and create their own relationships.

It can be daunting when you don't know what your child is doing, or what risks they may face. I once had a friend whose 13-year-old daughter, Suzanne, wanted to go to the mall and hang out with her friends on a Friday night. The problem was that Suzanne's mother didn't know any of these children or their parents. She wanted to tell Suzanne "no" but wasn't able to come up with a good enough reason other than it makes her uncomfortable. You don't have to have a reason. "No" means "no" and that's where the conversation needs to end. Parents should never have to make an excuse to keep their children safe.

As children move into middle school and on to high school, they meet new people and go through changes in style, outlook and social life. Don't be surprised one afternoon if they come home from school and ask you for a piercing. It is completely normal for their taste in movies, music and fashion to change as they develop their new identity. Disappearing into their room, spending endless hours on the phone and hanging out with friends—ones you've never met—are behaviors that signal their emerging identity. Along with this comes their need to challenge the way they're raised or your authority. Once this happens you have to hold firm on your boundaries and discipline. Children push the limits to see how far they can get and if you let up just one time it makes it that much more difficult to enforce the rules of the house.

The time in a child's life when he or she is searching for a peer group is vital because this group influences their behavior. Researchers at the University of Western Ontario conducted a study with two types of peer groups. The first group consisted of the cool and popular children while the second group had children who were considered as kind or nice and generally well thought of. The purpose of this study was to determine whether some peer groups are more influential than others.

This study monitored 526 Canadian children whose average age was 12, and identified 116 peer groups. The researchers looked at socially unacceptable behavior such as stealing and skipping school and asked the children to nominate classmates who were aggressive and antisocial as well as children who were nice to others and fun to be around. They were also asked to name who they liked the most and the least in their grade.

Over a three-month period, researchers discovered that the children were influenced by the behavior in their peer groups. This occurred much more among the popular groups than in the kind group of children. A child has a need to fit in with the "in" crowd which makes them much more likely to follow or go along. If, for instance, the popular child in school smokes, the chances are high that their peers smoke too because of a need for acceptance as well as pressure from the other group members.

Acknowledging that by early adolescence, peer groups have a significant influence on our children's behavior makes it that much more important for us to know who our children are associating with and what they are doing. True, being a part of the "in" crowd may make your child feel good and give them confidence but it also increases their odds of going along with the crowd and participating in inappropriate behaviors such as smoking, drinking, doing drugs or sexual activity.

Some children have such a strong desire to fit in that they'll do anything for acceptance. Look at gangs for instance. Why is it that so many children are willing to join such violent organizations? One reason someone joins a gang is that it offers what they aren't getting at home. Many children are susceptible to gang mentality because they've become detached from their families and it feels like no one wants or loves them. In a gang, at least they feel like someone cares for them. Gangs give children support and a reason to exist. Members always have the gang to support them emotionally or financially as long as they're loyal. Sadly, gangs offer exactly what many parent don't. Gangs are so close because many of the members are there for the same reason—the need for family and acceptance.

Friends begin to play a significant role during the teenager stage. This is a stage where the teenager will spend more time with friends than with the parent. During this time, they'll want to develop closer peer relationships to create a sense of belonging in the group. We need to play a role in supporting the teenager's needs but should set negotiable and non- negotiable boundaries to ensure a safe environment for our kids.

STEP AWAY FROM THE HERD

Parents usually wonder and ask why their children are involved in certain behaviors, when the answers are right in front of them. Their children don't have guidance, discipline or support at home. Parental guidance is very important to teenagers and young adults. At this age they are in a time of need. Teenagers at this age are trying to choose a road to take, and without the right guidance from parents they could take the wrong road and be lost forever.

Imagine you are on a journey. You have a vague sense of where you need to go, you have dreams and desires for your future but you're not sure how to see them fulfilled. You know you have family to turn to but you feel you need a friend—someone you could meet with in a coffee shop and talk to, someone who won't judge you and who will help you find your way. If you are a 'tween or teen this is likely your story. Their families tell them one thing, their friends another, the church something else and the media steamroller still another.

Most kids have significant leadership ability and clearly "have what it takes" for success but need someone to turn to. Most high school teens are concerned about their future vocational path and are searching to find their unique identities. Many rely on friends but few have seriously considered how the company they keep affects their future. We had just started home schooling Kyle last fall when the opportunity to go on Bob Proctor's cruise came up. We got the call on Wednesday evening offering us two tickets on cruise that would depart in three days from Fort Lauderdale, Florida. My husband and I were excited about the incredible opportunity, the chance to travel, meet new people and expand our thinking. After discussing all the benefits, we decided that Kyle would gain far more from the experience than we would. He would be able to meet other teens, network and expand his knowledge of the world, and I would get to spend some quality time with my 17-year-old, something that is very difficult to do at home. It was a win-win situation.

The cruise offered Kyle far more than I ever imagined. He met several teens that owned their own businesses and who were actively pursuing their dreams. He started talking about new possibilities and setting goals. We joined the Vemma group and he immediately began signing up new members. He was having so much fun that when we arrived at the various ports he didn't even want to get off. On the way home he talked non-stop about his plan and what it would take to get from where he was to where he wanted to be. He figured he could graduate high school a year early if he really worked hard. He was on fire. He was truly excited to get home and start making things happen.

His friends came over as soon as we got home to find out about the trip. He told them about what he had learned, shared his dream board and goals and introduced them to Vemma as a business. He was on top of the world. The next day he came home from his friend's house where he had spent the day. He said his friends couldn't believe that he had gone on a cruise and never gotten off to see the sights. They gave him a hard time telling him in great detail all of the fun things he had missed while away.

As planned, Monday he met with his home school administrator and arranged to accelerate his studies. His friends, who had also begun home schooling, made little comments about his work load both at school and home. They started showing up at the house at lunch time and then began hanging out anytime they could. They said things like, " It's stupid to kill yourself studying just to finish early", "Why do you always have to work?", " You should be having fun, it's your time to be a kid", "Nobody makes money on these businesses, except the people at the top", "You're just a teenager, you don't have to do it all now" and much more.

One week after returning from the trip, Kyle was sitting on the couch when I got home from work. He was quiet and withdrawn and when I asked him what was on his mind he said "nothing". When I pressed him he said, "it's too hard." When I asked him what was too hard? He said, "It's too hard to stay motivated, positive and hopeful when I'm surrounded by people who don't want me to grow or change."

Tony Robbins talks about how people will return time and again to his *Unleash the Power Within* seminars because of the way it makes them feel. They love the positive energy that leaves their minds, bodies and spirits energized, refreshed and vibrating at a very high level. He likens the experience to a rock concert, but I think it is much more spiritual than that. He says that it is possible to maintain the powerful feeling and the level of intensity after you leave, but few do because once they leave they are bombarded by negativity both internal (self talk) and external (peers, coworkers, spouse, parents, teachers, etc) that wears you down.

Tony Robbins believes in creating a plan each year to keep the momentum going throughout the year. Step one starts by asking you to write down the successes and amazing moments and things you loved from the previous year. If you have ever had to do this, you know how difficult it can be. I sat there for more than five minutes unable to think of anything. Instead, I thought of all of the missteps and bad decisions, would haves, should haves and could haves that filled my mind. I realized then that we are taught to focus more on what we do wrong rather than what we do right.

Jack Canfield, author of *Success Principles* also believes in recording your successes because, as he puts it, "Successes in the past will give you the self confidence that you can have more successes in the future." He encourages readers to keep a victory log—a simple list of daily successes that can be reviewed often, thus keeping your focus positive and wholly on success.

DECLARATION OF INDEPENDENCE

Some of the most significant people in a teen's life are those in his or her peer group. Kyle's story is a powerful example of this. The value and meaning that friends provide for a young person in the midst of identity formation can be life-changing. As your child begins to declare their independence their views of what is "cool" more than likely will collide with yours. Remember when you were young and had that feeling of invincibility? As you matured though, you realized that problems and challenges happen and as a result the idea that nothing bad can happen passes more with each birthday. I certainly don't believe that I'm invincible, but I do believe that we are all destined for greatness if we align ourselves with the right path. The same is true with our children. They may not always walk down the road that we want them to, but if we give them the map, their final destination will be success.

Today's youth are subject to so much more than we were as children. To make matters worse, when our children associate with friends who engage in drugs, alcohol, sex or any other harmful activities, it becomes easier for them to believe that such conduct is normal. Combine that idea with the feeling of invincibility and problems are unavoidable. Our children need to know our expectations of them and their behavior in no uncertain terms. If, for instance, they're to be home at midnight, then it is midnight not 12:01. Young people often are so focused on their personal world of friends and activities that our influence may seem to be squeezed out. We can't let this happen. We have to remain a constant focus in our child's life.

First of all, we need to make it clear to our children that they can't hang out with people we don't know. When we take the time to meet our children's friends, we get a good sense of their personalities, what they are "into" and their family situations. When I was young, I couldn't stay the night with any of my friends unless my mother called first to meet and make sure the parents were going to be home. As a teenager I thought I would die when she made those calls but now I do the same with my children. Make your home the hangout for your child's friends and welcome them to come over. Encourage your child to invite their friends over, so you can talk with them and get to know them better. There are many opportunities to learn more about our children's friends. Talk to them and ask them what they like about a friend or what they think of a situation. Use examples from your own experience. Spending time together and being involved in a child's life allows communication about friends and other sensitive topics to become natural and expected. Offer to drive your children and their friends to the movies, mall or a party. Take every step you can to make your presence known.

Words of caution though. Don't be too quick to judge your children's friends. Radical styles and unconventional appearances may be nothing more than a badge of identity. I have a friend who teaches history at a junior high school. On the first day of class one year, a young girl walked in dressed in black wearing black lipstick and make up. Greg instantly thought, "Oh great, an Emo, this is going to be fun." It turned out the Jessica was one of his best students and made straight A's all year long.

Along with your children's friends, get to know their parents as well. If you haven't met them, give them a call. Ask what their expectations are regarding curfews, sleepovers and behavior. Share your rules and views. Invite the friends' parents to contact you with any questions or concerns regarding the adolescents' behavior or to clarify arrangements for their activities. Doing so will add to your impressions of your child's friends. It will help you know here your child is, whom he is with and how they're being supervised when they're not at home. I found that some of my friends didn't have the same viewpoints as I did. They encouraged certain behaviors such as back talk and disrespect that I find intolerable and as a result, some of my relationships have changed too.

Realize that when you assert your presence and opinions your children may react negatively to any pressure or direct suggestions about whom they should hang out with. This is a strong sign that their friends aren't good influences. I've encouraged several of my children's friendships. In fact part of the motivation for some of my own friendships with parents was so that my children could meet their children. It's easy when children are young to control their friendships, but it becomes much more difficult to make sure they make wise choices in choosing friends when they get older. My advice to parents is to surround your children with other children they can be encouraged by later in life. Pick your children's friends—while you can—based on their parents. Look for people who share your values, share your discipline philosophy and are heading their children in the same direction you want your children to go. Then get your children around those children as much as you can. Doing so instills in your children with confidence to pick the right kind of friends now and skills that will carry over into other areas of their lives.

In addition to meeting our children's friends and getting to know their parents, I believe we should never assume our children are too smart to get into trouble. I remember one time during a parent teacher conference, one of the parents told me that "it couldn't be my child, he never does anything wrong. Besides, he knows better; we've had this discussion several times." Never assume your child is "too smart to drink" or "too moral to have sex" or "too afraid to use methamphetamines." I worked with numerous parents who talked openly about these issues with their children who swore they would never do "anything like that" or said "do you think I'm stupid? I know I can get pregnant." If you find yourself suspicious, follow your instincts, search their room and don't feel like you are invading your child's privacy. They don't have privacy when it comes to safety issues. You never know, you could be saving their life in the long run. It's better to have your child mad at you and safe than to see them hurt.

The need for acceptance is critical for children. Whether our children are young or teenagers, they long for acceptance and friendship. Fitting in is so important to our children that often they act and behave in ways they normally wouldn't. Outline expectations and rules clearly. Your child needs to know where you stand on behaviors like drinking, smoking, sex and dating. When older children attempt to fit in, they often engage in negative or risky behaviors that seem "cool." Knowing where you stand on these issues, and what consequences they face, decreases the likelihood that your child will engage in them.

Make sure your child knows that you are available to discuss social problems with them. Help to build their trust in you by listening to them. Show them the big picture. Sometimes children think that a certain clique or outfit is "do or die" for their social status. Explain how cliques and trends come and go, and stress the importance of making true, enduring friendships.

It is critically important to protect your relationship with the children so that you can maintain influence over them for the rest of their lives. This is not accomplished by giving them what they want, but by teaching them the difference between right and wrong. Too many parents allow too much freedom early and then try to get control back when the child tries to be an independent teenager. It should be the opposite. The time to gain control over a child's actions is when he or she is young, then a gradual release of authority is given to them as they get older.

The Importance of a Role Model

Anytime we want to make a success out of life, the first action we have to take is to find someone who is already a success in our chosen endeavor. Once we find that person, make it a point to talk to the following:

★ People who have made money in your desired field.

★ People who have lost money in your desired field.

★ People who have been in your field for years.

★ People who just recently started.

The teen years are a critical time for role models in your children's lives as well. Many teenagers have a difficult time talking to their parents, which is why finding a positive role model is so important. Even in the closest families, where communication is not a problem, there are some subjects — such as sex—that teens often feel more comfortable talking to another trusted adult about.

A recent study found a strong connection between teens and mentoring as well. Research conducted by SADD (Students Against Destructive Decisions) and Liberty Mutual revealed that teens who identify at least one influential mentor in their life have a higher sense of self and are more likely to take risks that affect their lives positively. In the study, 46 percent of teens with a mentor reported a high sense of self versus 25 percent of teens who did not identify with a mentor in their lives. More than half of teens reported that the absence of a mentor would negatively affect them.

Mentors can include family members (such as parents, aunts, uncles, and grandparents), other adults (such as teachers, guidance counselors, coaches, neighbors, and clergy) and peers—people who may have opportunities for interaction with some frequency. Teens reported these people to exhibit characteristics such as trustworthy, caring, understanding, respectful, helpful, dependable, fun, compassionate and responsible. This research is a call to action to adults to interact with teenagers—either in their professions or in their daily routines.

Children naturally look for role models to shape their attitudes and behaviors. As parents, it is important for us to make sure that they have plenty of positive role models. There are enough negative role models surrounding our children, from pregnant teeny bopper pop stars to athletes who use steroids. If we don't actively focus on positive role models, our children might seek advice from friends or adults who aren't the best influences. Parents have an obligation to guide, support and teach their children. A lack of parental guidance is not acceptable because it brings many unfavorable consequences. Parents should encourage their children to meet successful people who will motivate them to become someone that they want to become in life.

As your children grow, their circle of influence will naturally expand beyond you, the parent. This can be seen as a threat, but it is really a series of golden opportunities to see your kids blossom into well-rounded adults.

★

EXERCISE

Make a list of your role models and then out to the side write down the qualities that attracted you to them. Ask your children to do the same.

ROLE MODELS

PARENT

Name	Qualities

ROLE MODELS

CHILD

Name	Qualities

Chapter 9

Take Action Now

★

As parents, we are the role models for our children. If we're not living the best life we can, how can we expect our children to do so? We have to first focus on what we want, then accomplish our own goals and teach them to do the same when we are achieving our own dreams. When we discover the inherent good in each other and ourselves, we can then, as a family, experience an atmosphere at home which inspires everyone from parents to toddlers to teenagers, providing the perfect environment for success. Our abundance of resources allows us to create dynamic and continually evolving thoughts that impact the community and the world. It is important for us to have the capacity to dream and think beyond day-to-day realities, which allows us to make a difference within our lives, our children's lives, our community, and our world.

We are all role models or leaders in our own right and every one of us has something valuable to share. Our stories and our life experiences, when shared, can impact others on a highly personal level. We have the power to create change not only in our lives but in the lives of everyone we touch. This is accomplished when we first develop ourselves and strengthen our inner being. Only then do we have the confidence and ability to develop, inspire, empower and heal others.

I have learned some valuable lessons in the last few years. Lessons I believe, if shared, can help many people. When you reflect on your story, where is your focus? Is it on the crisis or on the process? We're all challenged at one time or another. How quickly we allow ourselves to move through these challenges depends largely on our focus. If you allow yourself to live in crisis mode, your mind will begin to "freeze" at a high stress point and you become stuck.

WHO ARE YOU?

Having always been interested in the power of the mind, I felt there was something missing very deep inside me—something I hadn't been able to access and clear by myself despite my best efforts. I decided it was time to take action to find a way of releasing a blockage that I knew intuitively was holding me back. I therefore attended a personal development seminar with Tony Robbins. During one of the exercises, he asked us to describe who we were. I had difficulty completing this exercise. Later that evening, I sat down and really thought about who I was. Words like detail-oriented, strict, and committed filled my paper. I knew these to be true but I wandered if there was anything I was missing, so I decided to ask my friends and family. Below is the email I sent to them.

> I have been working on a project and am having some trouble completing the assignment. I am putting together a list of my talents and need an outside perspective.

I thought who better to ask than the people who know me best. Would you please help me by sending a list of things you feel that I do well; my talents as well as a list of anything I don't do particularly well; my weaknesses. Any input will be helpful and greatly appreciated.

Love, Leslie

The response to my request from family and friends was overwhelming. I wanted to share just one of the responses so you can get an idea of how enlightening this process can be.

I wanted to get back to you. I don't know what kind of project you're working on, but know that it's not what you do but how you do it. You can do anything. Here are your personal Traits/Talents not in any particular order:

1. *Strength*
2. *Honesty*
3. *Decisive*
4. *Risk Taker*
5. *Independent*
6. *Action Oriented*
7. *Ethical*
8. *Trustworthy*
9. *Giving*
10. *Caring*
11. *Compassionate*
12. *Successful*
13. *Knowledgeable*
14. *Dependable*
15. *Friendly*
16. *Loving*
17. *Talented*
18. *Bi-Lingual*
19. *And More*

You probably don't need advice from me, but I know that everyone questions their purpose in life at one time or another. You have a made a difference in my life and have had a huge impact on the direction my life has taken. You have talents and personal traits that most people will never achieve. So, just be glad for what you have and who you are. Everything else is just BS. By the way, I didn't include a list of weaknesses because I don't think that word is a good reflection of who you are.

P.S. Your real talent is enjoying life…here's your sign:

Skills:

1. Bi-Lingual
2. Budgeting
3. Customer/ Person relations
4. Following Through / Goal Setting
5. Investing
6. Office leadership/ Management
7. Organizing
8. Researching
9. Saving
10. Scheduling
11. Shopping
12. Touring/Travel
13. Wine Expert
14. …on and on and on!!

Activities:

15. ATV/Motorcycle
16. Backpacking
17. Biking
18. Boating
19. Body Boarding
20. Camping
21. Court Sports
22. Diving
23. Exercising
24. Field Dressing Game & Fish
25. Field Sports
26. Fishing
27. Glassing
28. Hiking
29. Hunting
30. Ice-skating
31. Mapping/Course Directions
32. Off road racing
33. Road Biking
34. Rollerblading
35. Running
36. Scouting
37. Snorkeling
38. Snow skiing
39. Swimming
40. Walking
41. Water-skiing
42. Weight Training

What type of talents and weaknesses do you have? What I found amazing about this process was the differences between what I thought of myself and what others thought of me. I saw qualities that were hard and rigid while my friends and family saw entirely different traits. This is true for most of us. Others oftentimes see qualities we don't see, which is why I found this exercise valuable. It gave me a better insight into who I truly am. In the space below describe yourself and ask your children to do the same.

YOUR THOUGHTS

Now send an email to all of your friends and family and ask them to describe your talents and weaknesses. Take their answers and copy them in the space below. Circle the ones that are different and take a moment to think about why they see those qualities in you.

YOUR NAME:		CHILD'S NAME:	
Talents	Weaknesses	Talents	Weaknesses

EMAIL RESULTS

YOUR NAME:		CHILD'S NAME:	
Talents	Weaknesses	Talents	Weaknesses

VALUES

The majority of our parenting is directly linked to our values. Many of us take our values for granted yet our quality of life is guaranteed to improve dramatically by defining values and committing to live by them regardless of external circumstances. Studies have found that the most successful people live according to their top five values; and these are linked to the six human needs.

Tony Robbins says that everything human beings do, they do in order to meet one of six basic human needs, and we all share them. Values, beliefs, strategies and goals may vary, but our six human needs don't. These are often overlooked when it comes to our children. They have the same needs as adults. The first four, in no particular order, are fundamental needs; the remaining two—growth and contribution—are primary and essential needs.

1. Connection/Love
2. Certainty/Comfort
3. Variety
4. Significance
5. Growth
6. Contribution

All of these six needs are vital for us as humans, but Connection/Love is particularly important for children. We see this in their everyday life—especially teenagers. They want to fit in with the cool crowd and are willing to do whatever it takes to gain acceptance from their peers. Everyone needs to connect with others, to belong, to be accepted, to feel important, to be cared for and cared about and to give love as well as to receive it. If we're not creating a connection with our children and giving them the love they need, they'll find it someplace else.

trouble accepting those times when I didn't do what he wanted or give the approval or affirmation he needed so desperately. He lost his sense of what motherhood was and became boxed in emotionally.

In addition to children, some adults suffer from a lack of connection as well. For me, I had a personal struggle with connecting to anyone outside the family. My dad had a heart attack and my brother was paralyzed in an accident, which created strong bonds between us. I felt united with my family but couldn't get close to anyone else. I learned early on to take care of myself and others by helping my father and brother, but I didn't learn to count on anyone else. Before I met Rick many people described me as friendly but aloof. I had no clue until one day Rick pointed out to me that I don't take the time to analyze situations or acknowledge emotions. As a child and teen I did what was necessary to handle a situation. If for instance my brother needed help I helped him without thinking about the fact that he was paralyzed. I never grieved his accident.

When I married Rick he had three children and I learned quickly that life can be strained living this way. Children's lives are up and down. Add in hormones and you have a whole new set of dramas. I was no longer able to just move in and handle the situation. I had to explore not only their feelings but mine as well, which helped me to understand that one of my core beliefs and values was family. I had to change my behavior and stop internalizing so much. Many of us don't learn these until a tragedy happens, but we don't have to wait for extreme situations before we examine our inner lives. Look at your core beliefs and values and ask yourself if you're fulfilling the six basic human needs in a positive manner? If not, ask the question: "What would I need to believe, appreciate or do in order to fulfill my needs right now?" Do what's most important to you. Forget the rest because it's not adding value. Being busy for "busyness" sake is unproductive. When I was younger I even broke up with a boyfriend because he did not share my core values. He didn't want to spend time with my family, and I realized that we didn't place the same value on family and decided to end the relationship.

It's so important to know your values so you can live by them. You usually find that what you value in the outside world is a reflection of your internal values. Therefore I suggest you start by determining your "external values"—what you see around you. These are more tangible than inner values. Some examples of external values are:

★ A connected community

★ Healthy environment with pure water and clean air

★ Personal development tools to be taught in our schools

★ Making a contribution - assisting those less fortunate than ourselves

The mirror image of these values can be seen when looking at the corresponding internal values such as:

★ Continuous growth

★ Happy family life

★ Compassion, connectedness and empathy

Your core values could also include things that you're good at, and you're usually good at what you love. Imagine what our world would be like if everyone lived according to their beliefs and values. The next exercise, if done with an honest and open mind, reveals valuable insight as to where you are in life right now. Clarification around your values is the first step in building self-confidence, self-esteem and character. Commit to them and feel strong, capable and centered. Take whatever time you require to list your values in the space below, starting with the areas that are most challenging to you.

Review your list. Where have your values really been? Are you surprised at where you're currently directing your energy? Can you see a connection between how you're spending your time, and your results?

For most parents, their values don't always coincide with their children's values. Have you ever told your child to get up for school, only to be told she didn't feel well? Then shortly after you told them they can stay home from school, you see the look of relief on her face. Situations like this occur because there is a difference in values. They don't think school is as important as you do.

Value conflicts can cause problems in relationships. An excellent strategy is to sit down with your children and individually list all your values. Then compare notes, looking for commonality, and decide what five to seven values to commit to as a family. Be sure to discuss what you mean by the value too, because your interpretation of "discipline" for example, could well be different from your children's. This process takes the conflict out of decision-making because you have a foundation to work with. Stick to the values you've mutually committed to and watch your relationship flourish! Focus on what's important to you. Your values are the key to determining your child's values and whether or not they'll be successful in achieving them.

GIANT LEAPS

We have to take action now. We can't take baby steps because invariably too many distractions get in the way. As I always tell my children, "Don't wait. Make hay." The minute I made the decision to take action, my life moved forward by leaps and bounds. The moment you make the decision to do something about it and take action, get the wheels in motion. Looking back on my life I can see so many instances where such "miracles" have happened. I teach my children to live by this philosophy: "You don't have to know how to achieve your goals but you must take the first step." My mom used to tell me to "find a way to make it happen." This taught me that I had to do something, not just sit back and wait for things to happen to me. Some of the steps I've chosen to take are reading, visualization, then creating a vision board and a to-do list.

Read. Each of us has inherent talents and abilities; some are obvious, some have been lost or temporarily set aside and some have yet to be discovered. It is both your duty and obligation to identify your strengths, continuously hone your skills, stretch your imagination and open your mind to the endless possibilities in life. It does not matter where you are in the process, each day you have the opportunity to learn something new or reinforce knowledge already held. Knowledge is the key to success and education is mandatory. Start developing the skills you need to work smarter. If you develop the habit of learning and reviewing information frequently, you will remember more and be more effective in whatever you do. Your education will give you "the edge," for knowledge and experience will always lead to wisdom.

There are multiple paths to wisdom and many great resources such as books, audio CDs, seminars and mentors to educate and move you in the right direction. As you begin the process you will discover what works best for you, but you must begin. Allow yourself the luxury of reading and learning because the time you invest now will actually save you time and frustration later in life. You'll need both education and experience to win in life. The good news is you don't have to go it alone. By reading, you can learn from leaders who have traveled the road that you are now on. They have struggled, made mistakes and learned how to be successful. One of the greatest gifts leaders can give is to share their personal story, both triumphs and trials, because what you learn from their experiences will not only accelerate your education, but also lead you to your own personal wisdom.

I want to share with you a list of my favorite books, not a complete list by any means, just the ones that have had the greatest impact so far. Each book has had a positive impact on my life and my hope is that they will enlighten and encourage you in your journey as well. Of these books, I read some casually and some I chose to devote countless hours to their study. My initial goal was to read a book a month but once I began reading, I wanted more. I now read at least a book a week. If this sounds impossible to you, just start with ten pages a day. That's equal to a book a month!

Think and Grow Rich by Napoleon Hill

The 7 Habits of Highly Effective People by Stephen R. Covey

Zero Limits: The Secret Hawaiian System for Wealth, Health, Peace, and More by Joe Vitale

Raving Fans: A Revolutionary Approach to Customer Service by Ken Blanchard

How to Win Friends & Influence People by Dale Carnegie

Your Best Life Now: 7 Steps to Living at Your Full Potential by Joel Osteen

Battlefield of the Mind: Winning the Battle in Your Mind by Joyce Meyer

Awaken the Giant Within: How to Take Immediate Control of Your Mental, Emotional, Physical and Financial Destiny! by Anthony Robbins

Live with Passion! : Strategies for Creating a Compelling Future by Anthony Robbins (Audio CD)

Emerson: The Mind on Fire by Robert D. Richardson Jr.

The Angel Inside: Michelangelo's Secrets for Following Your Passion and Finding the Work You Love by Chris Widener

The Success Principles™: How to Get from Where You Are to Where You Want To Be by Jack Canfield

The Image by Chris Widener

Twelve Pillars by Jim Rohn

The Power of Focus: What the World's Greatest Achievers Know About the Secret of Financial Freedom and Success by Jack Canfield

7 Strategies for Wealth & Happiness: Power Ideas from America's Foremost Business Philosopher by Jim Rohn

The Difference Maker: Making Your Attitude Your Greatest Asset by John C. Maxwell

Maximum Achievement: Strategies and Skills That Will Unlock Your Hidden Powers to Succeed by Brian Tracy

The Purpose Driven® Life: What on Earth Am I Here For? by Rick Warren

Change Your Thoughts - Change Your Life: Living the Wisdom of the Tao by Wayne W. Dyer

What have you read lately? If you haven't picked up a book lately, don't feel bad; statistics show that most adults won't read a book once they graduate high school and a large percentage of those that start never read past the first few chapters. I was required to read so many texts in college that once I completed my coursework I had very little interest in reading anything other than fluff material. But that all changed a few years ago when my husband and I began a program of self-development.

As with anything new, the best way to become a master, whether it's in a business, a leadership role, a sport, a hobby or a concept, is through sequenced repetition. The more you read the more the ideas will start to take root in your subconscious mind. I have internalized the information I have read in these books and it has become a part of who I am. Reading, more than anything else, has given me the confidence and the words to share my story and connect to others on a much deeper level.

Visualization When you're on a mission to take action, there's no time for worry, doubt or fear. Become involved; fully engage the senses—see, hear, smell, taste and touch—feel the feelings of being the person you're choosing to become and attaining what you desire. We don't have to know how—each step unfolds as we take action, adapt to the changes, and expand our awareness. Visualization is such an important part of the process of realizing your dreams and we practice this skill with our children each day. The key to effective visualization is to remember that you already have your desire intellectually and emotionally. Whether we like it or not, expectations rule. We get what we expect rather than what we want. Many people don't see themselves as winners so they make no effort.

Vision Board Create a vision board, a collection of photos, images, words, sentences and affirmations supporting your dreams. Cover each important area of your life. The idea is to stimulate your mind, grab your attention and excite your senses as you see photos of yourself already in possession of your goal. Connect with your feelings and place your Vision Board where you'll see it daily, and set aside time to "be" with it. Also place affirmations and inspirational quotes on your Vision Board.

To-Do List Each morning over the next 21 days, list the six most important tasks for the day, prioritize them and take action. Start with the most difficult activity first—the one you would have procrastinated on! Visualize yourself completing all tasks with ease and feel the feelings of satisfaction. If for some reason you don't complete all six tasks, just transfer what's left to the next day's list and stick with the process. How many important activities will you achieve in a month—six months —a year?

Many of us wait for our plan to be perfect before we begin to take action. When is it perfect? Don't we learn from our imperfections? Isn't it our so-called "mistakes" that lead to growth? Constantly review your goals, dreams and to-do lists and take giant steps toward them. Remember that distractions lead to procrastination—the opposite of making a decision. Instead of allowing imperfections and uncertainties to distract you, make the best plan that you can and then start on step one, whether you're sure of what you're doing or not. You can correct mistakes as you go along but you will have no opportunity to correct things if you don't take action in the first place. So take your imperfect plan, take action and refine as you go. Looking back on your accomplishments and those of your children, you won't need to worry that your plan wasn't perfect to begin with. You will be able to bask in success.

---- ★ ----

EXERCISE

What is your story? Who are you influencing on a regular basis? Is it your spouse, your children, your employees, your co-workers, your community or is your circle of influence even larger? On the next page answer the following questions:

★ What's your story?

★ What are the lessons you have learned from that story?

★ And, how can your experiences help others facing a similar trail?

Use the space below for your answers.

★ What's your story?

★ What are the lessons you have learned from that story?

★ And, how can your experiences help others facing a similar trail?

CHAPTER 10

WRITE YOUR OWN RULES

$\bigstar$

Now you're ready to reinvent yourself and push forward, knowing that everything you need to succeed in life is already inside you. You need to have the confidence to write your own rules. I recently read an article published on CNNMoney.com about a group of people who have been writing their own rules for many years and are considered to be some of America's most successful entrepreneurs. They're not in Silicon Valley or Manhattan. Instead they live in the rural Amish enclaves. According to a 2009 report by Elizabethtown College Sociology professor Donald Kraybil, Amish businesses have a success rate of 95% compared to the average survival rate of 50% of businesses across the United States. The Amish aren't afraid of hard work, and they don't care what the rest of the country thinks of them, which distinguishes their success rate from the rest of the country. They stick to their values and write their own rules. I firmly believe in the same qualities that the Amish adhere to, such as hard work and discipline. Our children spend so much time letting others decide what's right for them—whether parents, the media or social networking, that they don't know how to think for themselves anymore.

Our children and most adults have forgotten how to be creative. With the advent of video games and the Internet, board games and play have gone by the wayside. Imagination is a vital skill that isn't taught in schools. Rick and I create each day, whether we are creating services or products for our business, books, speeches or other methods to get our message out into the world. My daughter carries a journal with her everywhere she goes and jots down notes about new inventions or how to make certain items better. She recently told Rick that he should make a series of videos teaching people how to repair cars and upload them to YouTube. She's ten and already filled several

K's Idea Book   2010

- Car repair tapes
- Massage back pack and other carry ons
- Pillows with tea
- Coffee mugs with battery to keep coffee hot
- Self opening house doors
- Butt pads for students with logos
- Cribs with vibration for babies
- Dog collars for little dogs - cute colors
- Gift box with 12 bookmarks & amazon gift card for 12 books.
- Flavor straws for water

journals with all of her great ideas. As I read through some of her ideas, such as a pillow with aromatherapy tea inside to help us relax, a massaging backpack, or a cup that heats coffee, I'm amazed at how creative and intelligent this 10-year-old is. To help your children do the same.

CREATIVITY

Life is about creation. I tell my children that we are in the business of creating. Creativity takes roots in our childhood, and for some reason often disintegrates as we mature. Like learning, staying in shape or maintaining a skill, creativity must be practiced and nurtured—in other words, use it or lose it. Life is an adventure for teens and adults too. Our experiences of creativity shape much of what we do in life. Creativity flourishes when actions are taken for enjoyment and in a stimulating environment marked by autonomy to explore and master skills necessary for future creative pursuits. We are all creative in one way or another andcapable of tapping into our own creative spirits. We have to stop overlooking our originality and imagination. To be creative, we need to set goals and think of unique ways to achieve them. I encourage my children to look for alternative avenues and to act differently from the way we have been. This helps them in going beyond the routine and conventional.

Creative people make more mistakes and are less proficient than more conventional types, yet they generate more ideas and success because they aren't afraid to step out of their comfort zone. Creative people are committed to risk. It is vital to our children's happiness (and our own for that matter) that we continue to grow and evolve. To do so we have to be willing to use our imagination and creativity. When we use the gift of imagination, we are inspired and we inspire others. This inspiration is the substance which allows us to become more and add more life to life.

Tapping into your creativity is only the first step. Many, perhaps most, people don't know how to apply their creativity and imagination to their own lives. To do so, we need to review our talents and strengths and follow our purpose in life. When we use the gift of imagination from the core of our true self, we are powerful creators with unstoppable visions. Through creativity and imagination, we can grow and evolve. When we figure out exactly how we want to live our lives, we are embarking on a journey to discover more about who we really are. So if you want to grow and help your children evolve into their own individual selves, use your imagination and teach them to do the same. Creativity is a great tool for personal development.

Many of us however, focus so much on working and getting ahead that we lose our creativity. Make a new rule to take time out to do something nice for yourself. Take your children along too. One day I took my daughter to get a pedicure and a lady sitting next to me was appalled that I would indulge her at such a young age. She spouted off about how her daughter wasn't ever going to have a pedicure until she was 18 because she didn't want her to feel entitled. I couldn't believe it, so in typical Leslie fashion I spoke my mind and let her know that I was teaching my daughter the value of rewarding herself for hard work and the importance of celebrating her successes. I was happy that she was able to learn this lesson at such a young age, one most adults have yet to learn.

Both activity and rest are necessary for our imaginations to work at their best. Look at nature, for example. Growth happens in the spring and summer. During the fall and winter seasons many plants and creatures rest. We have to take time for ourselves if we want to remain fresh, alive and responsive—and continue to grow and to evolve. I believe in hard work but I also believe it is necessary to rest so your work doesn't become stale. Even your heart rests after every beat. In fact, your heart is in its resting phase approximately 60% of the time.

Taking a "*me*" timeout is important because fresh and new ideas or "aha" moments often come at this time. When you revitalize your mind and body, you become:

★ Clear and open

★ Able to "hear" your intuition

★ Able to make better decisions and take action

A BENCHMARK FOR EXCELLENCE

The people who are the benchmarks for excellence are risk takers, creative and not afraid to be different. In our society, we're expected to conform, and different is frowned upon. People in ancient times went around in packs and outsiders were recognized as different and threatening to the well-being of the pack. I love the fact that we are all different from one another. Biologically speaking, we owe our mere existence to diversity, to uniqueness. Those best suited to the environment survive. What kind of world would this be if we were all the same? If everyone was the same, imagine how boring that would be. Differences are what make us all so interesting. Each of us has at one time or other met individuals that we realize "march to the beat of their own drummer." Some people consider this type of behavior as bad. This is especially true for teenagers. If you're not part of the right clique you can be ostracized. Look at how many teenagers commit suicide as a result of bullying.

I find the ability to be different to be a positive quality and encourage my children to be their own people and to cherish their individuality. Most people wish they had the courage to be themselves instead of just going along with the status quo.

"Marching to our own drummer" means not being willing to compromise values or ideals, because of what others consider the norm, or for the sake of being more popular. I want my children to be surrounded by people who like and accept them for who they are and don't expect them to change. Our differences move us forward. I have one friend who is very different. She is a social activist and many people don't like her. Rather than conform for the sake of conforming, she has her own unique view of life. We are polar opposites but I respect her individuality and find that her personality complements mine. People who "march to their own drummer" are many times the most interesting and stimulating individuals we'll ever meet.

Our children need to learn to look at people, attitudes, events and the world from a different perspective. When they're able to do this, they become thinkers and develop problem solving skills. Encourage your children to ask questions and stand up for what they believe in. I was listening to Rush Limbaugh the other day and I heard a story about a student in high school student who got into trouble for speaking his mind. His teacher was talking about politics and the importance of the need to be liberal and let everyone do what they like. This student disagreed and voiced his opinion, only to find himself sent to the Principal's office. Our children should never be chastised for having the courage to stand up for what they believe in.

Sit down with your children and review the list of their talents and strengths. Visualize with them what they can do differently to expand and grow these strong points. Instead of encouraging them to follow those who went before them, help them to take action and step outside of the norm. My goal for my children is to have others coming to them asking about their style, techniques or choices. Let's teach our children to strive for a point in life when people want to be like them and understand how it is that they do what they do, rather than the other way around.

Don't criticize, scorn or make fun of people who are different. Instead learn from them. Life has many great opportunities if we open our minds to the countless possibilities. Different is good. We should never pretend to be someone we're not. We are role models for our children so if we spend our lives living a false image, we're teaching our children to do the same. Diversity is what makes this world unique. We've all heard the classic definition of people who are described as "a square peg in a round hole." Sadly many of our children feel like this. They feel like they're watching the world from a different place. I have felt this way ever since I can remember—always slightly different. In many ways, it can be either a curse or a blessing; it depends on how you feel at the moment. I've tried to fight this feeling in the past because sometimes it can be depressing, but as time has passed I've learnt to accept it and live with it, and now I'm happier than most people I know. Instead of living inside the walls I climb over them.

MISTAKES OR OPPORTUNITIES?

It is important to learn to laugh at life and not take it so seriously. Life is meant to be fun and people who are different don't see problems—instead they view them as challenges. We need to learn from our mistakes, and the bigger the better. As a parent I spend a good deal of my time talking to my children. Sharing stories is an important part of my parenting style. I don't just share my success stories. I talk about the mistakes that I've made along the way, too—like the time when I lied to my friend only to get caught and lose her friendship.

My enthusiasm for sharing stories about my mistakes is sometimes lost on my children. They roll their eyes and say "Mom is going to try to teach about learning from our mistakes again." Granted, most of it is in good-hearted fun when they tease me, but they know deep down that the lessons are always valuable, even if they're not willing to admit it. Nobody likes to make mistakes but they are necessary teaching tools. Our brains are wired to learn from our mistakes according to a study by psychologists at the University of Exeter in England. The research concluded that our brains become more skillful based on the mistakes that we make throughout our lives. For some of us that means we're very skilled individuals!

The three names on the next page are famous people who learned from their mistakes and become very successful include:

★ Abraham Lincoln. He lost numerous elections before becoming the President of the United States.

★ Steve Jobs. He was once fired by Apple Computer. Now he's CEO.

★ Madam Curie. Her discovery of radiation was a mistake. We wouldn't have X-rays or CAT scans today without her.

Our children, up until they leave the home, are limited in their experiences so we have to be willing to share our stories with them. Even if they don't appear to be listening, they are. The most memorable stories tend to be those we can identify with at a personal level.

When we learn from our mistakes and view them as challenges or opportunities, we're essentially creating our own personal toolbox of solutions. With each new mistake we add a new tool that we can carry with us throughout life. One of the best tools I've taken from my mistakes is gratitude. Each time I fall I know the value of my climb back up, and thus appreciate my success that much more. Don't be afraid of your mistakes or afraid for your children to make them. Let them spill the milk or toss a red shirt in with a load of whites. The milk can be wiped up and you can always buy new underwear and socks. Embrace mistakes and learn from them. And share what you know.

One of the main things that can hinder us from recovering from our mistakes and reaching our goals is an inability to be flexible. Life changes, and we have to be able to adapt. If I were to ask you to describe a strong object, you would more than likely refer to something made of metal or concrete. A car for example, or a set of weights or a dam. Yes these are strong, but are also susceptible to breaking. Think about a car accident. The metal doesn't bend, it gets crushed. An earthquake-proof building, on the other hand, sways with the movement of the ground. Ironically, true strength and staying power comes with the ability to be flexible and adapt to whatever life has to offer.

Our children need to learn that when they make a mistake it is not the end of the world. They have to be able to adapt and look for alternative avenues to reach their goals. The idea that strength equals rigidity is outdated. If you have been burdened by mistakes in the past, learn from them, forget about them, move on and adapt a new way to accomplish what you want. Our children can't focus on their mistakes or they'll never move forward. Treat your mistakes and theirs as lessons, and apply them as learning references in future endeavors. If you're afraid to fail then you risk all your chances to achieve your goals in life. Trying gives you a 50% chance of succeeding, while failing to take action assures that you will fail.

But when you try, make sure you follow through. I've seen so many children set a goal and then fail to take all the steps needed to accomplish it. You may have the drive to start but not the motivation to persist through the difficulties. If this is the case, you'll never have the life you want. Instead you'll sit on the sidelines and watch others pass by. Obstacles and problems are going to happen and your world is going to change, so you have to be flexible and ready to adjust to new situations.

We all make mistakes and that's okay. The problem is often that we are too hard on ourselves. To quote a friend of mine, "Snap out of it." You can and will recover from them. The fear of making a mistake does not have to stop you from trying. In life, our children will encounter difficulties. They'll receive criticism or even be regarded as being "different" or "strange" by other people. Don't let this discourage them. Continue to strive for success and the world will be yours for the taking.

Children require an intentional investment of time and energy over the long term. Growing up well does not just happen. We have to model the correct behavior for our kids. If someone doesn't agree with how you parent, that is their problem. I know that Rick and I have friends who think we're too "mean." We don't care what they think because we write our own rules for parenting and we're not going to hold our children up to higher standards than we hold ourselves.

Children grow up so fast that before you know it, your days of having a controlled, direct influence over them will be over. Rick and I were at dinner the other evening talking about our oldest son and how much progress he's made. He improved when Rick finally told him, "I can't be here for you financially. I will offer emotional support and advice, but you have to take authority over your own life." Once Rick clarified the rules, Daniel took responsibility and changed for the better. As parents, we often begin to lose control of our children as they enter junior high school. It doesn't have to be that way if we can give them a strong foundation, clarify our rules and require personal responsibility from them.

BE MORE, EXPERIENCE MORE, HAVE MORE

Hard work pays off, so if you need to sacrifice something for a better cause, do it. If you have to miss your favorite TV show, so be it. Our children are so "me" focused. They want anything and everything. By giving them the encouragement to focus on others and give back, they can grow and reach beyond the mentality that they currently have. Our primal instincts lead us to satisfy our own desires first, which is why it is so important to make a conscious effort to help others and teach our children to do the same. We need to extend ourselves beyond our own perceptions.

Personal growth is about a process of giving and receiving. Giving is a virtue. You know that it is better to give than to receive, but for many people receiving is just so much more fun. My daughter and I frequently visit a relative who is in an Alzheimer's unit. At times my visits are made out of obligation. This unit is a secured area and very depressing. I don't always feel like going, but my daughter doesn't mind at all. She is such an inspiration to me. She'll tell me we need to go and see the "people who don't feel well." To my amazement, one day she wrote in her journal about helping them. She wanted to take fingernail polish and make up and give them a spa day one Sunday afternoon. The amount of self sacrifice she was willing to make to help these people made me realize how proud I am of her and that all children have the capacity to give. We as parents just need to encourage it.

Each Christmas, our children give up something to make room for their new gifts. One year my daughter wanted a new IPod. I asked her what she was going to do with the old one. She went in her room, cleaned it up, wrapped it, and asked me if I could take her to the local children's home so she could donate it to one of the children living there. Our sons do this as well. One year we gave them new bikes and, without us asking, they replaced the tires and grips on their old bikes and donated them to the teenage children at the home. Through sacrifice and giving, my children have been able to see what life is like for those children in the foster home, which makes them appreciate all they have.

Some time ago a friend of mine's daughter developed an attitude of entitlement. Nothing was good enough. She wanted designer clothes and didn't want to help around the house.

My friend decided that, rather than lecture on deaf ears, her punishment would be to work at a local charity for a month to help sort coats and clothes for less fortunate children. As the time passed, her daughter's attitude changed. When the month was over, she not only realized how fortunate she was, but also decided to stay and help on a regular basis. Our children need to see that their lives are not so bad after all. When they realize that there is always going to be a child who has less than them, it puts their lives into perspective.

In addition to teaching them to give and sacrifice, we need to give our children hope. Having hope, and teaching your children to have hope, is an important part of the fundamental growth of your children. The amount of hope we give them determines how our children view the world. Being able to have hope in our future is important, especially in today's society. As children grow, they are influenced by many things that cross their paths, such as their parents' words and actions, things that happen in school and relationships with other adults. All these experiences, both good and bad, create the thought processes that follow them throughout their adult lives. Instilling hope as they mature into young adults is very important because it instills confidence in them, even when they fail. Teaching children to have hope in their own ability builds confidence, and that is the first step in being able to act upon their abilities.

Our actions create the daily influences that determine the mindset of our children. To have consideration for others and be honest in your intentions is what makes children grow into honorable adults. Having hope allows them to view what happens on a daily basis in a non-judgmental way. The lack of hope creates bitter attitudes and allows the blame game to begin. All we have control over is ourselves. As parents, we have control over our children's development. With hope, our children have faith, trust, love, and the certainty that all things are indeed possible.

The desire to have, to acquire and to possess is present in all of us. However it does not often generate the satisfaction and fulfillment that we imagine. By contrast, giving to others, contributing to worthwhile causes and creating new ideas or products will bring us even more than we can imagine— more financially, more spiritually, more physically, more intellectually and more in relationships. In the end, we are the chief determiners of our happiness. What do you have in you?

Too many parents are giving their children too much power to make decisions on their own too early in life. Our children should never dictate what we do. Parenting is not about pleasing our children. When we do this, we're teaching them to depend on others and they won't learn how to fend for themselves in the real world. Freedom and giving in to our children is now mainstream parenting. We need to focus on teaching and disciplining our children in an attempt to build their characters and sense of responsibility.

Our job is to plant within them the desire to do well and to write their own rules in this world. One of my favorite quotes is "Two things we give our children. One is roots. The other is wings." We have to give our children deep enough roots so they can decide which direction their wings are going to take them.

★

EXERCISE

Create an idea journal and write ideas in it every day. Have your children do the same.

www.ingramcontent.com/pod-product-compliance
Lightning Source LLC
Chambersburg PA
CBHW031601110426
42742CB00036B/639

9 7 8 0 9 8 6 7 7 6 2 7 4